W9-BMQ-236

Read Me

I AM MAGICAL

Open Me and I Will Reveal
12 Secrets to Love, Happiness & Personal Power.
As You Leaf Through Me See How Remarkable You Feel.

This book has powerful, positive subliminal messages embedded within it.
Master of Thought Collection.

ALINKA RUTKOWSKA

Applauded by scientists, doctors and business people, this book is an exhilarating experience stretching your mind to a whole new dimension. **THE AUTHOR**

Editing by Chris Horton
Background image by Eren Ülsever
Author photograph by Paulina Dziubińska

ISBN: 1451594364
ISBN-13: 9781451594362

What I am about

We are what we think. All that we are arises with our thoughts. With our thoughts, we make the world.[1]

If you've enjoyed other books on reality creation, you'll love this. Even if you've disliked other books on reality creation, you'll still love it. What you hold in your hands is the documented scientific research behind reality creation, including a workbook. You are the magician of your life. It is your show and, by mastering your thoughts, you create everything in it. This book dissolves the fog surrounding the reality creation phenomenon and provides you with a set of tools to make it work for you.

This book is a guided tour of the intricate mechanism of your thoughts, teaching you how to master it in such a way that you attract into your life the love, joy, wealth, health, youth, peace, beauty, wisdom and power you desire.

The message at the heart of *Read Me – I Am Magical* is that everything you wish for in your life already exists – in your mind, and that there is a universal law that can transform this into reality in your day to day life. Just like gravity, this law applies to everything and everyone. But what is still not clear to most people is how to put it into practice. By the time you finish reading this book, however, you will possess all the skills and knowledge you will need to master this magical law and change your life forever.

The information and techniques found in this book are not taught in any school, or in any middle or higher education facility, although the author believes they should be among the very first things we learn. Now they are in your hands, you have the power to make remarkable use of them. You now have all it takes to make the magic work.

Just by opening this book and leafing through its contents – without reading more than a few words – you have taken your first step to becoming an empowered creator of your world, whether you know it or not. It's not what you read that will have the most impact on you, however. It is the subliminal messages hidden in the book that make the read a truly exhilarating experience.

What advertisers have been doing for decades – influencing your choices without your conscious participation – is being applied in this book – though this time, you are informed. This work provides you with life-changing insights interwoven with powerful, positive subliminal messages that flow directly into your subconscious, which does not judge and has no sense of humor. Your subconscious mind will not argue. Your subconscious mind will take this seed for granted and direct your conscious mind to grow from it a beautiful plant. Enjoy.

Man's mind, once stretched by a new idea, never regains its original dimensions.

Neither will yours.

Read Me – I AM MAGICAL

Believe nothing just because a so-called wise person said it. Believe nothing just because a belief is generally held. Believe nothing just because it is said in ancient books. Believe nothing just because it is said to be of divine origin. Believe nothing just because someone else believes it. Believe only what you yourself test and judge to be true.

BUDDHA

Dedication

To you, dear Master of Thought – wishing you an exciting journey as you discover the pages of this book.

To you, dear Critical Observer – inviting you to verify for yourself the content of this book and to share your judgment.

To you, dear Magician of Life – with gratitude for attracting this book to your reality.

BLESSINGS OF LOVE AND JOY.

Acknowledgements

Is it even possible to identify all the contributors to this book?

I would love to thank all the scientists and researchers who spend their days and nights experimenting with reality creation methods and translating their discoveries in order to enlighten the world.

I thank all the great philosophers who have left a legacy in the form of books and quotes, all of which are so inspiring in our quest for the truth.

And, on a more personal note, I would like to thank the incredible people I am surrounded by for their inspiration and support.

My brother Tomek, the first reader, whose enthusiasm for this endeavor motivated me to explore further and further.

My boyfriend Burak, whose support and belief in my ability to complete this book were unshakeable.

My friend Agnieszka, who was always there for me to discuss my theories and who shared with me the excitement of getting this work ready for publishing.

Table of Secrets

Table of Exercises

Preface

The preeminent mental limitation that humankind has imposed on itself is the belief that our lives are mainly shaped by states of consciousness, circumstances and coincidences beyond our control. I believe this is untrue.

We are what we think. All that we are arises with our thoughts. With our thoughts we make the world.

The source of all our reality is our own thoughts. The book you hold in your hands is dedicated to proving this point via studying and mastering the intricate mechanism of our own thoughts, which leads us to achieving whatever we desire.

Why do we start in October? Well, think of this as a university course – the academic year usually starts in this month. There is more to it than this, however. I have been interested in the power of the mind since I was a small child, although I first started systematically writing things down in October 2008. This process lasted for around a year. I then focused on my main themes, before expanding on them and, finally, transforming them into a book for the benefit of a wider audience.

October - Awareness

You see but you do not observe.

SIR ARTHUR CONAN DOYLE

Sherlock Holmes: *You have frequently seen the steps which lead up from the hall to this room.*
Dr Watson: *Frequently.*
Sherlock Holmes: *How often?*
Dr Watson: *Well, some hundreds of times.*
Sherlock Holmes: *Then how many are there?*
Dr Watson: *How many? I don't know.*
Sherlock Holmes: *Quite so! You have not observed. And yet you have seen.*

SELF-AWARENESS

In order to be powerful, we need our senses to be working at their fullest potential. We tend to behave like Dr Watson in the dialogue shown above: we "see", yet we do not "observe". Awareness of self is crucial because it enables us to recognize who we are and to spot any unhelpful patterns we may have developed. Having understood those negative patterns we might be clinging to, we can change them. Awareness is the starting point of any change. If we are not aware that something is wrong, then we will never change it. We must be aware of ourselves; we must not only see but also observe.

In order to observe and be aware of ourselves, we need to ask ourselves questions related to our senses, thoughts and feelings. The following is a very helpful exercise that can greatly increase our powers of awareness.

EXERCISE 1: AWARENESS

At some point during the day or night, take time to ask yourself the following questions:

1. *What am I seeing?*
2. *What am I hearing?*
3. *What am I smelling?*
4. *What am I tasting?*
5. *What am I touching?*

And subsequently:

6. ***What am I thinking?***
7. ***What am I feeling?***[7]

Questions 6 and 7 are extremely important because, as we will learn, thought accompanied by feeling is the key element of reality creation.

Later, try to recall the exact moment you asked yourself these seven questions, and bring to mind the sensations you felt in response.

Repeat this often. This exercise will trigger the power of awareness, which in turn will trigger telepathic and intuitive faculties.

Awareness is the starting point of all reality creation endeavors; and the foundation for developing psychic awareness, as well as many other magical qualities, is meditation.

MEDITATION

The gift of learning to meditate is the greatest gift you can give yourself in this life. For it is only through meditation that you can undertake the journey to discover your true nature, and so find the stability and confidence you will need to live, and die, well. Meditation is the road to enlightenment.[8]

How many thoughts are there running through your mind in a given moment? A lot. Think about it. Look at your watch and measure how much time you actually spend focusing on just one thought – not very long. This persistent chaos in our heads gives us little opportunity to focus on any one thing, let alone our real selves. Meditation is an amazing technique that allows us to look into ourselves – our real selves – and to listen to our inner voice. It also enables us to get in touch with our higher consciousness and to achieve inner peace and a deeper understanding about the world around us. Furthermore, as the gateway to focused reality creation, we can use meditation to control and create our lives on all levels: physical, material, mental and spiritual.

Derived from the Eastern world, meditation is an ancient technique that has been used for centuries by sages, magicians, witches and monks whose works testify to its powers. Adaptations of the Eastern meditation techniques are increasingly being practiced in Western culture.

SCIENCE OF MEDITATION

Meditation has attracted substantial interest from scientists, who are now able to use new technologies to see exactly what goes on inside the brains of individuals who practice meditation. Research has shown that regular meditation actually alters the way the brain is wired, and that these changes could be at the core of claims that meditation can improve health and wellbeing.[9]

Recent research indicates that meditating, even for just ten minutes, can have dramatic effects. Several studies have demonstrated that the brains of people who meditate, even for a short time, generate a higher frequency of alpha waves (electromagnetic waves produced by a relaxed brain) and experience less anxiety and depression.[10]

To discover which part of the brain is most influenced by meditation, researchers at Harvard Medical School used high-resolution magnetic resonance imaging (MRI) technology on participants to monitor their brain activity as they meditated. They concluded that meditation activates those sections of the brain responsible for the autonomic nervous system, which in turn governs bodily functions that conventional medical science tells us we have no conscious control over. These include digestion and blood pressure – which are all too often adversely affected by stress. The conclusion was that modulating these functions could help to ward off stress-related conditions such as heart disease, digestive problems and infertility.[11]

It is claimed that meditation may also increase the volume of so-called grey matter in your brain – a major component of the central nervous system. This was the conclusion of researchers at the University of California, Los Angeles, who also used MRI to scan the brains of people who practice meditation. In this study, the researchers reported that certain regions in the brains of long-term meditators were larger than those in members of a control group. Specifically, they showed significantly larger volumes of regions known for regulating emotions (the hippocampus and areas within the orbito-frontal cortex, the thalamus and the inferior temporal gyrus). "We know that people who consistently meditate have a singular ability to cultivate positive emotions, retain emotional stability and engage in mindful behavior," said Eileen Luders, lead author and a postdoctoral research fellow at the UCLA Laboratory of Neuro-Imaging. "The observed differences in brain anatomy might give us a clue why meditators have these exceptional abilities," she added.[12]

A separate study, published in *Psychosomatic Medicine*, involved a randomly selected group of 90 cancer patients. They were taught mindfulness (a type of meditation). After seven weeks, those patients who had practiced meditation reported that they felt significantly less depressed, anxious, angry and confused than did members of the control group, who hadn't meditated. The meditators also seemed to have more energy and had fewer heart and gastrointestinal problems than did the other group.[13]

Another study concluded that positive emotions such as loving, kindness and compassion can be triggered through meditation. The subjects in this study were asked first to concentrate on their loved ones and to wish them wellbeing and freedom from suffering. After some training, they were asked to generate such feelings towards all beings without thinking about anyone in particular. Using functional magnetic resonance imaging (fMRI), scientists concluded that through training, people can develop skills that promote happiness and compassion.[14]

Other health benefits associated with meditation include better sleep, lower blood pressure, improved immunity and the ability to stay centered and calm in stressful situations. Meditation helps us to do less yet accomplish more.[15]

Brainwave patterns visibly alter during meditation. Before meditation, a normal person has unbalanced brainwave patterns. After 15 minutes, both brain hemispheres become synchronized in deep meditation. After 25 minutes, and continued synchronization, the benefits are infinite.[16]

The benefits of meditation are limitless, but let's name just a hundred:[17]

PHYSIOLOGICAL BENEFITS:

1. Lowers oxygen consumption.
2. Reduces respiratory rate.
3. Increases blood flow and slows heart rate.
4. Increases tolerance to exercise.
5. Enables deeper levels of physical relaxation.
6. Reduces blood pressure.
7. Lowers blood lactate levels (raised levels can cause anxiety attacks).
8. Eases muscle tension.
9. Helps alleviate chronic conditions, including allergies and arthritis.
10. Reduces symptoms of premenstrual syndrome.
11. Assists post-operative healing.
12. Enhances the immune system.
13. Reduces activity of viruses and emotional distress.
14. Boosts energy levels, strength and fitness.
15. Helps with weight loss.
16. Reduces number of free radicals and minimizes tissue damage.

17. Boosts skin resistance.
18. Reduces cholesterol levels, lowering risk of cardiovascular disease.
19. Improves flow of air to the lungs, resulting in easier breathing.
20. Slows the ageing process.
21. Raises levels of DHEAS (dehydroepiandrosterone).
22. Prevents, slows, or controls pain associated with chronic diseases.
23. Makes you sweat less.
24. Cures headaches and migraines.
25. Increases orderliness of brain functioning.
26. Reduces need for medical care.
27. Boosts energy efficiency.
28. Makes participants more inclined to get involved in sports and other activities.
29. Significantly relieves asthma symptoms.
30. Improves performance in athletic events.
31. Normalizes our optimum weight.
32. Harmonizes our endocrine system.
33. Relaxes our nervous system.
34. Produces lasting beneficial changes in brain's electrical activity.
35. Cures infertility (the stresses of infertility can interfere with the release of hormones that regulate ovulation).

PSYCHOLOGICAL BENEFITS:

36. Builds self-confidence.
37. Increases serotonin levels, which affect mood and behavior.
38. Helps resolve phobias and fears.
39. Helps control thoughts.
40. Helps with focus and concentration.
41. Increases creativity.
42. Increases brainwave coherence.
43. Improves learning ability and memory.
44. Increases feelings of vitality and rejuvenation.
45. Increases emotional stability.

46. Improves relationships.
47. Reduces rate of mental deterioration.
48. Makes it easier to cut out bad habits.
49. Helps develop intuition.
50. Increases productivity.
51. Improves relations at home and at work.
52. Enables you to assess situations with greater clarity and perspective.
53. Helps you to ignore superfluous issues.
54. Increases ability to solve complex problems.
55. Purifies your character.
56. Develops will power.
57. Improves communication between the two brain hemispheres.
58. Helps you react more quickly and effectively to stressful situations.
59. Improves perceptual ability and motor performance.
60. Boosts growth rate of intelligence.
61. Increases job satisfaction.
62. Increases the capacity for intimate contact with loved ones.
63. Decreases susceptibility to mental illness.
64. Improves social interaction.
65. Reduces aggressive tendencies.
66. Makes it easier to quit bad habits such as smoking or excessive drinking.
67. Reduces need for, and dependency on, drugs and/or medication.
68. Makes you need less sleep.
69. Helps you to fall asleep more easily; can help cure insomnia.
70. Increases sense of responsibility.
71. Reduces road rage.
72. Decreases restless thinking.
73. Decreases tendency to worry.
74. Increases listening skills and empathy.
75. Helps you to make more accurate judgements.
76. Increases tolerance levels.
77. Gives you composure needed to act in considered and constructive ways.
78. Helps you to develop a stable, more balanced personality.
79. Boosts emotional maturity.

SPIRITUAL BENEFITS:

80. Helps you keep things in perspective.
81. Provides peace of mind; is a gateway to happiness.
82. Helps you discover your purpose.
83. Increases self-actualization.
84. Increases compassion.
85. Increases wisdom.
86. Facilitates a deeper understanding of yourself and others.
87. Harmonizes body, mind and spirit.
88. Encourages a deeper level of spiritual relaxation.
89. Increases acceptance of oneself.
90. Helps you to learn forgiveness.
91. Changes attitudes to life.
92. Creates a deeper relationship with the spiritual world.
93. Allows you to attain enlightenment.
94. Improves ability to focus on your inner self.
95. Helps with living in the present moment.
96. Creates a widening, deepening capacity for love.
97. Allows you to discover the power and consciousness beyond the ego.
98. Allows you to experience an inner sense of knowingness.
99. Allows you to experience a sense of oneness.
100. Increases synchronicity in your life.

MEDITATION IN VARIOUS SPIRITUAL MOVEMENTS[18]

Meditation is a component of many religions. It is also practiced outside religious traditions. Let's look at the aspect of meditation in major religions:

Buddhism – Buddhist meditation is mainly concerned with transforming the mind and using it to explore itself and other phenomena.[19] The historical Buddha, Siddhartha Gautama, was said to have achieved enlightenment while meditating. In Buddhist mythology, there were 28 Buddhas, all of whom used meditation to achieve spiritual progress.

Christianity – Christian traditions include various practices that can be identified as forms of meditation. Monastic traditions are the basis for many of these. Catholic practices such as the rosary and the adoration (focusing on the Eucharist), or the Hesychast tradition of prayer in Eastern Orthodoxy, are all comparable to forms of Eastern meditation that focus on an individual object.

Hinduism – The earliest specific references to meditation in Hindu literature state that "having becoming calm and concentrated, one perceives the self (*atman*) within oneself".[20] *Yoga*, one of the six orthodox schools of Hindu philosophy, focuses on meditation. The word "yoga" is derived from the Sanskrit *yuj*, which means "to control, yoke or unite". It refers to techniques and disciplines of asceticism and meditation that lead to spiritual experience. Yogic practices help to control the mind and senses so the ego can be transcended and the true self (*atman*) experienced, leading to *moksa* (liberation).

Islam – A Muslim is obliged to pray five times a day: once before sunrise, at noon, in the afternoon, after sunset, and once at night. During prayer, a Muslim focuses and meditates on God by reciting the Qur'an and engaging in dhikr to reaffirm and strengthen the bond between Creator and creation. This guides the soul to the truth. Such meditation is intended to help maintain a feeling of spiritual peace. The Islamic prophet Muhammad spent long periods in contemplation and meditation. It was during one such period that he began to receive the revelations of the Qur'an.

Judaism – The Jewish mystical tradition Kabbalah is inherently a meditative field of study. The Talmud teaches that the scholar has an advantage over the prophet because he develops an understanding that is both intellectual and conceptual, allowing the scholar to think more deeply and communicate his wisdom to others. The advantage the prophet has over the scholar lies therefore in the transcendence of his intuitive vision. The ideal illumination is achieved when the insights of mystical revelation are brought into conceptual structures. Corresponding to the learning of Kabbalah are its traditional meditative practices. For the Kabbalist, the ultimate purpose of its study is to understand and be at one with the Divine.

Of all the self-improvement techniques within the psychic and spiritual fields, meditation is by far the most effective. It is also the most simple.[21]

So far, we have learnt how science acknowledges meditation and how it is present in all major religions. We have also looked at the incredible properties of meditation. Now to answer the million dollar question: how to meditate? There are numerous resources available, including books, DVDs and study programs. Ultimately, however, the best way to learn is the way that works best for you. After all, you know better than anyone how to get in touch with your inner self. According to Roger Thomson, PhD, a practicing psychologist and Zen meditator, there is a sure fire way to know if the method you have adopted is right for you: "If you're feeling better at the end, you are probably doing it right"[22].

The following meditation exercise is one I find extremely effective; one which has allowed me to achieve many of the physiological, psychological and spiritual benefits listed earlier.

EXERCISE 2: MEDITATION

Environment

Make sure you are undisturbed.

Posture

Different spiritual traditions, and different teachers within those traditions, prescribe or suggest different physical postures for meditation, including sitting, flat on your back, and standing postures. Perhaps the most famous are cross-legged sitting postures such as the lotus position as in figure 1. However, any position that is comfortable for you will be correct – providing, of course, that your spine is straight and you are not slouched.[23]

Figure 1. Meditation[24]

MEDITATION PART 1 [25]

1. Allow the head to fall forward on the chest. Breathe deeply in and out three times. Return to the upright position.

2. Allow the head to tip fully backwards. Breathe deeply in and out three times. Return to the upright position.

3. Tip the head as far as possible to the left. Breathe deeply in and out three times. Return to the upright position.

4. Tip the head as far as possible to the right. Breathe deeply in and out three times. Return to the upright position.

5. Allow the head to fall forwards, then move it in an anti-clockwise circle three times.

6. Repeat the last exercise, moving the head clockwise three times. Return to the upright position.

13

..uthe in through the nose with a number of short, sharp intakes until the lungs are full. Hold it a moment, then suddenly exhale through the mouth with a "huh" sound. Do this three times.

8. Breathe in slowly and fully through the right nostril (hold the left one closed if necessary), feeling the stomach balloon out as you do so. Hold it a moment, then exhale slowly through the mouth, flattening the stomach as you do so. This exercise moves all the stale air from the bottom of the lungs. Do this three times.

9. Repeat the last exercise, this time breathing in through the left nostril and out through the right nostril. Do this three times.

If you were sitting, now you can lie down (keeping the spine straight).

MEDITATION PART 2 [26]

Relax your body while breathing deeply. As you inhale and exhale, do the following:

1. Release all tension from your legs, starting with your toes and the soles of your feet, then move upwards, relaxing your ankles, calf muscles and shins. Relax your knees, then focus on your thighs.

2. Relax your hips and waist, your abdomen and lower back, then move up the spine to your upper back. Relax your lungs and chest.

3. Relax your shoulders and arms, elbows, wrists, hands and fingertips.

4. Relax your head and all the muscles in the neck. Relax your jaw and face muscles. Relax your eyes and forehead. Release all tension from the crown of your head.

5. Scan your body. If you feel any remaining pockets of tension or pain, imagine, as you breathe, that your breath is connecting with the tension elsewhere in your body and is taking that tension away as you exhale.

6. *Relax your mind. Let any thoughts, worries or concerns from the day drift away as you exhale.*

7. *Release any unwanted feelings, emotions and memories as you exhale.*

8. *Look into yourself and find inner satisfaction and peace of mind.*

Later on, we will introduce other exercises that include affirmations or visualizations, but for now, don't think about anything; just relax.

MEDITATION END

For your physical well-being, it is important that you end each meditation period with a re-awakening of the physical and conscious selves. This should be done in the reverse order to the method for relaxation (our part 2).[27]

Command each section of your body to awaken refreshed, vibrant and healthy.[28] Alternatively, if you are meditating before bedtime, command each section of your body to stay relaxed and gain strength during the night. By doing this, you will awaken refreshed, vibrant and healthy.

Once you have mastered this basis of meditation, you can start creating variations that address your needs and wants at any given moment.

In this first meditation exercise we let our mind wander freely. This moment, however, is the moment of power and this power can be released both by affirmation and visualization. These are ultimately the tools of reality creation.

AFFIRMATION

Affirmations are words or phrases that are said over and over in order to affirm thoughts about our reality. Such affirmations help trigger the subconscious mind into action. It is often said that a lie repeated enough times eventually becomes the truth. Well, what you are affirming is not a lie, just a future state that you are enabling to happen. Clearly, if a lie can become the truth, then your affirmation is bound to succeed!

During our lives, we think and say things to – and about – ourselves over and over again. Through sustained repetition, these thoughts form beliefs that in turn become our reality. In this way, we develop fears about a host of issues, such as money, illness, our bodies, and relationships. However, since we created these realities, we also have the power to change them.

Affirmations are positive statements recited in the present tense with attention, desire and conviction. So, if you want to be richer, your affirmation should be "I am rich", not "I will be rich" or "I am not poor". "I will be rich" is not as effective because it implies that this will happen in the future, and since you are in the "now", what you are seeking will always elude you. "I am not poor" is also incorrect. Although the use of the present tense is correct in this statement, the negative use of the word "not" has no place in an affirmation, which should always be positive. If you were to use this statement as an affirmation, your mind would resist focusing on the "not" and just absorb "I am poor", which would clearly be a counterproductive exercise.

Affirmations are messages sent to your higher consciousness and to the universe. When we become convinced we can create reality in a certain way, then we can. Doubt is the only obstacle in reality creation, so doubt should be removed. Affirmations can be repeated at any time – for instance, while you're waiting in line at the supermarket checkout, in the car, or taking a shower. However, they are most powerful when repeated during meditation on an inhale-exhale basis. Below is an affirmation meditation I love to do.

EXERCISE 3: AFFIRMATION MEDITATION

Bring yourself to a meditative state, but then, instead of just letting your mind wander, inhale and say: "I am", then, as you exhale, say whatever it is you desire. I say "(inhale) I am (exhale) divine perfection", or "(inhale) I am (exhale) love and joy" or "(inhale) I am (exhale) bliss and peace". You can affirm whatever it is you desire and be sure that the universe will conspire to make it happen.

VISUALIZATION

A visualization, which works in the same way as an affirmation, is a mental picture of a desired state, and is especially powerful when accompanied by a feeling. For example, if you aspire to be wealthy, you could imagine yourself flying first class en route to an exotic holiday, or checking out your bulging bank account. If you are convinced that this is (to become) your state, then there will be an added frisson of excitement that will help the universe guide you to it.

Of course, the best results are achieved when we practice visualization during meditation. Consider the following:

EXERCISE 4: VISUALIZATION MEDITATION

Bring yourself to a meditative state and then, instead of just letting your mind wander, visualize whatever it is you desire, hold the picture in your mind for a while and then release it, allowing the universe to conspire to make it happen.

"We are what we think. All that we are arises with our thoughts. With our thoughts, we make the world."[29] Therefore, rid your mind of any negative thoughts such as failure, disease, inadequacy or poverty. Your thoughts are messages to the universe. Whatever you fill your mind with is transformed into your reality. Everything is energy and energy cannot be destroyed, only transformed. Consequently, positive thoughts will be transformed into a positive reality and negative thoughts into a negative reality. Controlling your thoughts creates the reality you desire.

HARM NO ONE

If you have tested what is written above and judged it to be true, you have just equipped yourself with one of the most powerful reality creation tools. This way of creating your world is true magic. You are power. You can create anything. But having realized this, bear in mind that in reality creation there is but one rule:

E'er it harm none, do as ye will.[30]

You can create anything you desire as long as you do not harm anybody, including yourself. Clearly, the definition of "harming" is open to interpretation. But if, for example, you want to make two people fall in love with each other (this could simply entail visualizing them together living happily ever after), you should ask them for their permission first. However, if your friend tells you she really wants to be happily married, you can do the mental work of attracting the right partner to her without selecting a specific person.

THE WHERE, WHEN AND HOW OF MEDITATION

The where

You can meditate anywhere, but ideally it should be somewhere where you can relax and where you won't be disturbed. Be sure to wear comfortable clothes, or none at all, and switch your mobile phone off. You might find meditating somewhere outdoors, like at the seaside or on a mountaintop, especially powerful, but you can also train yourself to meditate in less glamorous settings, such as at the office, on a plane or train, or in the car (as a passenger!).

The when

Day or night?

The best time to meditate is the time that feels most natural and comfortable to you. You might find yourself to be more receptive at night when the moon is out and you can light some candles. I tend to find meditation to be most powerful just before I go to bed. This time of the day – just before your unconscious mind awakes and your conscious mind goes to sleep – is a good time to get in touch with your higher self. In this receptive state, your mind can be commanded to reveal the answer to a particular question, either while you sleep or immediately upon waking.

The how

A good way to start meditating is by trying, and customizing, established techniques until you find one that works best for you. Listen to your body and let your inner self guide you.

You may choose to meditate in silence or with a musical accompaniment. If you choose the latter, make sure you pick music that enhances your experience and isn't too distracting. You might also seek to increase your mental powers by using music with subliminal messages that communicate directly with your subconscious mind, bypassing your conscious judgment (see July – Subliminal Messages).

Magic is creating your reality via meditation, affirmation and visualization. It all boils down to mental work. However, this mental work can sometimes turn out to be something quite unexpected. You might have summoned so much energy that you suddenly feel the urge to dance or jump up and down. You may feel like you are living in some kind of parallel universe. And it might feel great. However, at some point you'll want to come back to the "real" world or get rid of all this energy. The removing of excess energy is called grounding.

EXERCISE 5: CAKES & ALE

Cakes & Ale refers to grounding[31] – to moving from the magical world to the reality we live in. This process is designed to show our appreciation of the great mental abilities we have been blessed with, as well as to get rid of the excess energy that we have raised during our mental work. As the name suggests, it traditionally involves having something to eat and drink – cake

19

and ale, for example. But you could opt instead to touch the ground with your palms to release the spare energy into the earth. Alternatively, you might choose to have sex, work out, or go to sleep. "Cakes & Ale" means "good things in life", so choose something that makes you feel good!

November – Gratitude

Whenever we are appreciative, we are filled with a sense of well-being and swept up by the feeling of joy.[32]

M.J. RYAN

The last day of October is when Halloween is being celebrated by people of all faiths. Halloween has roots in the Celtic festival of Samhain, which celebrates the end of the "lighter half" of the year and the beginning of the "darker half", thus marking the Celtic beginning of the New Year. It was said that on this day the border between this world and the Otherworld grew so thin that the spirits were able to pass through.[33] This belief has influenced numerous cultures around the world, which, as a result, have come to celebrate and remember the dead.

Some people might consider this to be a time of sadness, a time to shed tears as we remember loved ones who have passed away. For me, it's a time of reflection and a time to express gratitude for every moment we live, for every person we encounter, for every gift we receive, every lesson we learn, and for every smiling face we see.

Let us express gratitude – it's the gateway to happiness.

GRATITUDE IN SCIENCE

"Over the past quarter century, unprecedented progress has been made in understanding the biological, psychological, and social bases of human emotions. As psychologists further unravel the complexities of emotions, gaps in understanding are revealed. One of those gaps concerns the psychology of gratitude. A distinguished emotions researcher recently commented that if a prize were given for the emotion most neglected by psychologists, gratitude would surely be among the contenders. In the history of ideas, the concept of gratitude has had a long life span, but in the history of psychology, a relatively short past. For centuries, gratitude has been portrayed by theologians, moral philosophers, and writers as an indispensable manifestation of virtue – an excellence of character. For example, gratitude is not only a highly prized human disposition in Jewish, Christian, Muslim, Buddhist and Hindu thought, it is deemed an unrivaled quality in these traditions, essential for living life well. The consensus among the world's religious and ethical writers is that people are morally obligated to feel and express gratitude in response to received benefits. For example, Adam Smith, the legendary economist and philosopher, proposed that gratitude is a vital civic virtue, absolutely essential for the healthy functioning of societies."[34]

Gratitude has been defined in a number of ways throughout history. The German philosopher Immanuel Kant described it as "honoring a person because of a kindness he has done us". Scottish philosopher Thomas Brown defined gratitude as "that delightful emotion of love to him who has conferred a kindness on us, the very feeling of which is itself no small part of the benefit conferred". German theologian Dietrich Bonhoeffer wrote: "In ordinary life we hardly realize that we receive a great deal more than we give, and that it is only with gratitude that life becomes rich."[35]

"Gratitude is a prayer. It is a joyful and selfless expression of thankfulness from within. Whenever you are in a state of gratitude and appreciation you are focusing your thoughts and energy on the beauty and abundance that is already present in your life. You are sending a clear message to the universe that this is what you would like to experience more of. There is no greater prayer than one of sincere heartfelt love, appreciation, and gratitude. These pure emotions are of the highest vibrational frequency, and through the law of attraction they will automatically attract even more to be thankful for. They will create a vibrational match for all the beauty and abundance that the universe has to offer."[36]

Gratitude, like any other phenomenon, can be explored from various angles. The Buddhist word for gratitude, *katannuta*, consists of two parts: *kata*, which means "that which has been done" – especially "that which has been done to oneself", and *annuta*, which means "knowing or recognizing". *Katannuta* therefore translates as "knowing or recognizing what has been done to one" or, more precisely, "knowing and recognizing what has been done to one for one's benefit". While gratitude has emotional connotations (we "feel" grateful, for example), *katannuta* is more intellectual, more cognitive. The sort of gratitude implied by this word involves an element of knowledge of what has been done to us, or for us, for our benefit. In short, if we do not know that something has benefited us, we will not feel gratitude.[37]

So, again, it all boils down to awareness (see October – Awareness). When you are aware of all the wonderful things in your life, you can be grateful for them and when you are grateful, you become attuned to this high vibration, which in turn attracts more of these good things (see April – Reality Creation).

Although gratitude is something that anyone can experience, some people seem to feel grateful more often than others. People who tend to experience gratitude the most also tend to be happier, more helpful and forgiving, and less depressed than their less grateful counterparts.[38]

"Through quantum physics we now know that everything there is, is vibrational matter. All matter is energy made up of sub-atomic particles and atoms. Through this unified energy field, our thoughts resonate and project. Based on our feelings, emotions and thoughts, this determines our vibration frequency that is broadcast from us out into the universe. This is our own unique, vibrational signal. It is the personal signature that we resonate that is answered and returned to us."[39]

Physicists have discovered that there is an awful lot of empty space within even the most solid-looking objects. Similarly, there is a growing consensus that the events and circumstances of our lives unfold in much less unpredictable and haphazard ways than previously thought. These misapprehensions have occurred because our perception of the world

23

is obtained through the decidedly unreliable filter of our five senses. In reality, everything is comprised of particles moving in a constant dance of energy. At times, these particles collide and either ricochet off in another direction or fuse together into different forms with different characteristics. All of this happens in accordance with the thoughts that have formed them – the very thoughts that are going on in your own head.[40]

Without thoughts to form them, these particles are merely inert ingredients in a universal soup, waiting around to be formed into something by your mind. Your mind is constantly pulling apart and rearranging this energy to construct the life you experience. If you are unaware of this, or unaware of the power you have to affect matter with your mind, then you may carelessly allow thoughts and their embodied energies to flow around in your head without any order. This can cause experiences in your life to happen that you would certainly never have consciously chosen.[41]

GRATITUDE BY ANCIENT HAWAIIANS[42]

The ancient Hawaiians well understood the power of gratitude, which they have been practicing for many centuries through blessings. They concluded that the secret for attaining true health, happiness, prosperity and success is to:

Bless everyone and everything that represents what you want.

This secret is at the heart of the Aloha Spirit. Not only does this describe the attitude of friendly acceptance for which the Hawaiian Islands are famous, it also refers to a powerful way to resolve any problem, accomplish any goal, and to achieve any state of mind or body that you desire.

In the Hawaiian language, aloha means much more than just "hello" or "goodbye" or "love". Its deeper meaning is "the joyful (oha) sharing (alo) of life energy (ha) in the present (alo)".

24

As you share this energy, you become attuned to the universal power that the Hawaiians call "mana". The loving use of this incredible power is the secret for attaining true health, happiness, prosperity and success.

The way to tune into mana and have it work for you is remarkably simple, but to gain its full benefits, you should practice it regularly and frequently. ***Bless everyone and everything that represents what you want.*** That's all there is to it. Clearly, though, something so simple needs explaining.

To bless something means to give recognition or emphasis to a positive quality, characteristic or condition, with the intent that what is recognized or emphasized will increase, endure or come into being.

Blessing is effective in changing your life or getting what you want for three reasons:

- First, the positive focus of your mind stirs up the positive, creative force of the power of the universe.
- Second, it moves your own energy outward, allowing more of the power to come through you.
- Third, when you bless for the benefit of others instead of directly for yourself, you tend to bypass any subconscious fears about what you want for yourself.
- Also, the very focus on the blessing acts to increase the same good in your life.

What is so beautiful about this process is that the blessing you do for others helps you as well.

Blessing may be done with imagery or touch, but the easiest and most common way to do it is with words. The main kinds of verbal blessings are:

Admiration – This is the giving of compliments or praise to something good that you have become aware of. For example, "What a beautiful sunset; I like that flower; you're such a wonderful person."

Affirmation – This is a specific statement of blessing for increase or endurance. For example, "I bless the beauty of this tree; blessed be the health of your body."

Appreciation – This is an expression of gratitude that something good exists or has happened. For example, "Thank you for helping me; I give thanks to the rain for nourishing the land."

Anticipation – This is blessing for the future. For example, "We're going to have a great picnic; I bless your increased income; Thank you for my perfect mate; I wish you a happy journey; may the wind be always at your back."

To gain maximum benefit from blessing, you will have to give up or cut down dramatically on the one thing that negates it: cursing. This doesn't mean swearing or saying "bad" words. It refers to the opposite of blessing: criticizing instead of admiring; doubting instead of affirming; blaming instead of appreciating; and worrying instead of anticipating with trust. Whenever you do any of these things, they tend to cancel out some of the effects of blessing. So the more you curse, the harder it will be and the longer it will take to reap the rewards from a blessing. On the other hand, the more you bless, the less will be the harm you cause by cursing.

EXERCISE 6: BLESSINGS

Practice the ancient Hawaiian technique that leads you to true happiness: ***Bless everyone and everything that represents what you want as often as you can.***

Here are some ideas for blessing various needs and desires. Apply them as often as you like, as much as you want.

Health – *Bless healthy people, animals, and even plants; everything that is well made or well constructed; and everything that expresses abundant energy.*

26

Happiness – Bless all that is good, all the good that is in all people and all things; all the signs of happiness that you see, hear or feel in people or animals; and all potentials for happiness that you notice around you.

Prosperity – Bless all the signs of prosperity in your environment, including everything that money helped to make or do; all the money that you have in any form; and all the money that circulates in the world.

Success – Bless all signs of achievement and completion (such as buildings, bridges, and sports events); all arrivals at destinations (of ships, planes, trains, cars and people); all signs of forward movement or persistence; and all signs of enjoyment or fun.

Confidence – Bless all signs of confidence in people and animals; all signs of strength in people, animals and objects (including steel and concrete); all signs of stability (like mountains and tall trees); and all signs of purposeful power (including big machines, power lines).

Love and Friendship – Bless all signs of caring and nurturing, compassion and support; all harmonious relationships in nature and architecture; everything that is connected to or gently touching something else; all signs of cooperation, as in games or work; and all signs of laughter and fun.

Inner Peace – Bless all signs of quietness, calmness, tranquility, and serenity (such as quiet water or still air); all distant views (horizons, stars, the moon); all signs of beauty of sight, sound or touch; clear colors and shapes; the details of natural or made objects.

Spiritual Growth – Bless all signs of growth, development and change in nature; the transitions of dawn and twilight; the movement of the sun, moon, planets and stars; the flight of birds in the sky; and the movement of wind and sea.

The previous ideas are for guidance if you are not used to blessing, but don't be limited by them. Remember that any quality, characteristic or condition can be blessed (e.g. you can bless slender poles and slim animals to encourage weight loss), whether it has existed, presently exists, or exists so far in your imagination alone.

Serge King, the author of *The Little Pink Booklet of Aloha*, which contains the above theory, not only explains the Aloha Philosophy, he also describes having used the power of blessing to heal his body, increase his income, develop skills, create a deeply loving relationship with his wife and children, and establish a worldwide network of peacemakers working with the aloha spirit.

EXERCISE 7: PIKOPIKO – ENHANCING YOUR POWER TO BLESS[43]

There is a technique practiced in Hawaii that enhances your power to bless by increasing your personal energy. It is a simple way of breathing that is also used for grounding, centering, meditation and healing. It requires no special place or posture, and may be done while moving or still, busy or resting, with eyes open or closed. In Hawaiian, the technique is called "pikopiko", because "piko" means both the crown of the head and the navel.

The technique

1. Become aware of your natural breathing (it might change on its own just because of your awareness, but that's okay).

2. Locate the crown of your head and your navel by awareness and/or touch.

3. Now, as you inhale, focus your attention on the crown of your head; and as you exhale, focus your attention on your navel. Keep breathing this way for as long as you like.

4. When you feel relaxed, centered, and/or energized, start to imagine you are surrounded by an invisible cloud of light, or an electro-magnetic field, and that your breathing increases the energy of this cloud or field.

5. As you bless, imagine that the object of your blessing is surrounded with some of the same energy that surrounds you.

———

Think about what you feel inside when you are grateful for something. You feel good, happy, blessed, sometimes thrilled and excited. In turn, this embodied gratitude radiates the energy of happiness and satisfaction. If you focus on that feeling and thought, it will expand and enhance that vibration, and what you are thankful about today will create even more things to be thankful about and appreciate tomorrow.

HOW DO WE KNOW THIS TO BE TRUE?

A number of scientists have theorized that what we are aware of we draw to us and draw ourselves towards. We do this by forming mental structures, which align the necessary energies to allow that particular experience to flow through our senses. When we project energy within, it creates a structure that, within a short period of time, manifests itself externally. This is how gratitude brings us more of what we want. Simple. If today we project the attitude of gratefulness onto a cent, tomorrow we will have a dollar to be grateful for.[44]

If you think about your life and all the things you like about it, you will notice how blessed and lucky you are. Praise and appreciate everyone and everything in it and all those things you like will grow and expand, bringing you more things to be grateful for.[45]

We have a lot of things to be thankful for: the beautiful sunshine that warms our face; the rain that feeds the plants and gives life to the planet; beautiful music; works of art; thought-provoking paintings; fulfilling jobs – or if our work is not fulfilling, our awareness of both this and the power we have to change it. And let's not forget our family and friends who are always there to support us when we need them, or the strangers around us who are all our potential friends, or even potential family! Let's be thankful for our present partners, and for future partners that are yet to manifest. I shall let Buddha's words sum up my feelings:

Let us rise up and be thankful, for if we didn't learn a lot today, at least we learned a little, and if we didn't learn a little, at least we didn't get sick, and if we got sick, at least we didn't die; so, let us all be thankful.[46]

In this world of energy, nothing stays the same: everything is constantly changing. Our gratitude is creating energy that allows the mind to focus upon the models in our subconscious that form the basis of our preferences, which expand and multiply to form improved versions of themselves. Remember that this law is always at work, whether we are aware of it or not.[47]

Even if you are not a scientifically minded person, there are plenty of compelling, non-scientific reasons why you should cultivate an attitude of gratitude:[48]

First of all, a grateful attitude promotes the cherishing of life's positive experiences. By consciously taking pleasure in the delights of life, you will be able to achieve maximum satisfaction and enjoyment from your current circumstances. There was a time when I used to feel a bit down whenever my boyfriend went away for long periods. But by cherishing every word of our phone conversations when we were apart and by valuing every moment spent together, I came to learn that the times we were together were all the more intense and emotionally charged because of, not despite of, those lengthy periods of separation. And I have also learnt to make the most of the moments when I am alone by dedicating myself to sports, reading, writing or socializing, and by never taking for granted the great times we have when we are together.

Second, expressing gratitude bolsters self-worth and self-esteem. You become so much happier when you realize how much other people have done for you or how much you yourself have accomplished. I think about how, when I was a little girl, my parents helped me to become the woman I am today, and I am also thankful to myself for the self-development I enabled on the way to becoming who I am today.

Third, gratitude helps us deal with stress. More precisely, the ability to appreciate your life circumstances may be an adaptive coping method by which you positively reinterpret stressful or negative experiences.[49] Furthermore, research suggests that traumatic memories are less likely to appear (and are less intense when they do) in those who are regularly grateful.[50] Expressing gratitude during challenging moments, as hard as it might be, can help us adjust and move on.

Fourth, expressing gratitude encourages moral behavior. You are more willing to help others because you become aware of kind and caring acts and feel compelled to reciprocate. You are also less likely to be materialistic because you appreciate what you have and become less fixated on accumulating things.

Fifth, gratitude helps us to build social bonds, strengthen existing relationships and nurture new ones.[51] Keeping a gratitude journal (see exercise 9) is a good way to increase feelings of connectedness with others. Several studies, described later in this chapter, have shown that people who feel gratitude towards certain individuals experience closer, stronger relationships with these people.

Sixth, expressing gratitude tends to inhibit invidious comparisons with others. When you are genuinely thankful for what you have (family, friends, home, etc.), you are less likely to be continually comparing your own life to other people's and striving to make sure you are "keeping up with the Joneses".

Seventh, the attitude of gratitude is incompatible with negative emotions: it dissolves negative feelings like anger, bitterness, greed, jealousy and fear. It's hard to feel guilty, resentful or infuriated when you're feeling grateful because gratitude creates only positive feelings: love compassion, joy and hope. As we focus on what we are grateful for, fear, anger and bitterness melt away, seemingly effortlessly.

Last but not least, gratitude prevents us from taking the good things in life for granted. Because we are extremely adaptive beings, it's all too easy for us to adjust to positive life circumstances without stopping to appreciate what a true blessing they are.[52]

Someone once asked the artist Georgia O'Keeffe why she magnified the size of small objects such as flower petals – making them appear larger than life – and reduced the size of large objects such as mountains – making them seem smaller than life. "Everyone sees the big things," she replied. "But these smaller things are so beautiful, and people might not notice them if I didn't emphasize them." That's the way it is with gratitude and letting go. It's easy to see the problems in our lives;

they're like mountains. But sometimes we overlook the smaller things and fail to notice how beautiful they are.[53]

So, what would you be doing if you had all you desired? You would be expressing your gratitude. And, because like attracts like, the powerful emotion of gratitude will attract more of what you are grateful for.

EXERCISE 8: ATTITUDE OF GRATITUDE

Make a conscious decision to have an attitude of gratitude. Choose to live in a state of constant joy, gratitude and appreciation, and acknowledge how fortunate you are. Don't take even the simplest things for granted – appreciate them and give thanks. Being a living embodiment of gratitude is good for you: it increases your sense of wellbeing, awareness, enthusiasm, happiness, determination, and optimism. It raises your vibrational frequency and sets in motion a process of ever-increasing joy, gratitude, and abundance.[54]

Professor of psychology at the University of California-Davis, Robert Emmons has long been interested in the role gratitude plays in our physical and emotional wellbeing. He and Professor Michael McCullough, of the University of Miami, conducted a study[55] that required several hundred people in three different groups to keep daily diaries. The first group recorded the events that occurred during the day, while the second group noted their unpleasant experiences. The remaining group made a daily list of things they were grateful for.[56]

The results of the study indicated that daily gratitude exercises resulted in higher reported levels of alertness, enthusiasm, determination, optimism and energy. Additionally, the gratitude group experienced less depression and stress, was more likely to help others, exercised more regularly and made more progress toward personal goals. According to the findings, people who feel grateful are also more likely to feel loved. McCullough and Emmons also noted that gratitude encouraged a positive cycle of reciprocal kindness among people, since one act of gratitude tends to encourage another.[57]

McCullough says these results seem to show that gratitude works independently of faith. Although gratitude plays a substantial role in most religions, he believes the benefits extend to the general population, regardless of faith or lack thereof. In light of his research, McCullough suggests that anyone can increase their sense of wellbeing and create positive social effects just by counting their blessings.[58]

THE LAW OF GRATITUDE

The *Science of Getting Rich*, by US author Wallace Wattles, claims that "the whole process of mental work to getting what you desire can be summed up in one word: gratitude. First, you believe that there is one Intelligent Substance, from which all things proceed; second, you believe that this substance gives you everything that you desire, and third, you relate yourself to it by a feeling of deep and profound gratitude". The author goes on to suggest that many people who order their lives correctly in all other ways are kept in poverty by their lack of gratitude. Having received one gift from God, they cut the wires connecting them to Him by failing to make acknowledgment. The more gratefully we fix our minds on the Supreme when good things come to us, the more good things we will receive, and the more rapidly they will come. The reason for this is that the mental attitude of gratitude draws the mind closer to the source from which the blessings derive.[59]

"There is a Law of Gratitude, and it is absolutely necessary that you should observe the law if you are to get the results you seek. The Law of Gratitude is the natural principle that action and reaction are always equal, and in opposite directions. And if your gratitude is strong and constant, the reaction in Formless Substance will be strong and continuous, the movement of things you want will always be toward you. You cannot exercise much power without gratitude, for it is gratitude that keeps you connected with Power."[60]

———

"Success is a skill. Happiness is a skill. Gratitude is a skill. Like all skills, they must be practiced clumsily before they can be done naturally. So, if you'll devote ten honest days to the practice of feeling true gratitude and happiness, I can promise you a dazzling new skill. A skill that just naturally attracts success, like a magnet draws iron. Because nothing attracts good fortune and success like a joyous, grateful heart."[61]

EXERCISE 9: GRATITUDE JOURNAL

From the earliest cave paintings, through clay tablets, papyrus sheets, hieroglyphs etched on pyramid walls, stretched goatskin, to modern paper, the written word has always had a sense of ... *permanent importance* ... about it.[62]

Dedicate a few minutes every day to writing down all the things you are grateful for. Be specific, and try not to repeat the same things over and over again. When you decide to create a different list every day, your mind will be focused on spotting those wonderful events and people you can be grateful for, thus aligning you with the high gratitude vibrations. Your Gratitude Journal, which should be for your eyes only, can be paper-based or electronic and can include photographs and souvenirs. Make sure you really feel the gratitude before you commit these feelings to words. This is a truly wonderful and powerful tool you are creating. Read your journal regularly and observe the feelings this creates in you.

The Gratitude Journal exercise is a terrific way to get attuned with the joyful appreciative vibrations, however the ultimate gratitude exercise is the one that directly creates whatever we desire. As previously described, our subconscious mind does not distinguish between the past, the present and the future. We have learned that whatever we give thanks for multiplies, so **the ultimate reality creation method is to be thankful for what we desire**. I call it the "Thank you in advance" exercise.

EXERCISE 10: THANK YOU IN ADVANCE

What is it that you desire? Imagine that you already have it. Imagine yourself looking at it, touching it, smelling it. Feel the joy and gratitude it inspires. Hold it in your mind and release this thought to the universe, knowing that your desire is shortly to be manifested.

———

Thank you for reading this chapter, blessed be you and your spiritual growth.

December – Love Vibrations, Unconditional Love

Infinite Love is the Only Truth, everything else is Illusion.[63]

DAVID ICKE

We are told that "love is all around us"[64] and that "all you need is love"[65], but have you ever stopped to consider what love actually is?

According to the dictionary[66], love is "any of a number of emotions related to a sense of strong affection and attachment". Love can refer to a variety of different feelings, states and attitudes, ranging from generic pleasure ("I loved that meal") to intense interpersonal attraction ("I love my husband"). This diversity of uses and meanings, combined with the complexity of the feelings involved, makes love unusually difficult to consistently define.

As an abstract concept, love commonly refers to feelings of intense, tender care for another person. However, even this limited definition of love encompasses a wealth of different feelings, from the passionate desire and intimacy of romantic love and the non-sexual emotional closeness of familial and platonic love[67] to the profound oneness or devotion of religious love[68]. In all its various forms, love acts as a major facilitator of interpersonal relationships and, owing to its central psychological importance, is one of the most common themes in the creative arts.[69]

The ancient Greeks had a sophisticated appreciation of this complex emotion and developed a range of different words to describe its many forms and nuances:[70]

Eros is passionate love, combined with sensual desire and longing. From this word, the English noun "erotica" derives, as does the modern Greek word "*erotas*", meaning "(romantic) love". However, *eros* not only refers to love of a sexual nature, it also describes love that goes beyond *philia* – the love shared between friends – to encompass emotions associated with romantic relationships. This definition was refined by the Classical Greek philosopher Plato who argued that although *eros* starts as a feeling for another person, it can evolve to include an appreciation of the beauty within that person, or even an appreciation of beauty itself. It should be noted that Plato did not consider physical attraction to be an essential component of love – hence the modern use of the word "platonic" to mean "without physical attraction". He also said eros helps the soul recall knowledge of beauty and contributes to an understanding of spiritual truth. Throughout history, lovers and philosophers have sought truth through *eros*. The most famous ancient work on the subject is Plato's *Symposium* (see February – Loving the One 1), which takes the form of a discussion between Plato's teacher Socrates and his students about the nature of *eros*.

Philia translates as "friendship" in modern Greek. Developed by Plato's student Aristotle, it describes a dispassionate, virtuous love that encompasses feelings of loyalty to friends, family, and community that requires virtue, equality and familiarity. In ancient texts, philos denotes a general type of love that exists between family members, friends and lovers, as well as a desire or enjoyment of an activity.

Storge means "affection" in ancient and modern Greek. It is natural affection, like that felt by parents for their children. Although rarely found in ancient texts – when it was used almost exclusively to refer to relationships within the family – it has since been used to describe a feeling of acceptance, or tolerance, of a situation, i.e. "loving the tyrant".

Thelema in ancient and modern Greek describes the desire to do something, to be occupied, or to be in a position of prominence.

Xenia means "hospitality", which was extremely important in ancient Greece. The word was used to describe the almost ritualistic friendship between a host and his guest – both of whom may have been complete strangers before having met. In return for food and shelter, the guest was expected to repay the host with gratitude. The importance of this type of friendship is evident throughout Greek mythology; the best examples perhaps being Homer's *Iliad* and *Odyssey*.

Agape means "love" in modern Greek. In ancient Greek, it often referred to a non-specific feeling of affection, rather than the attraction suggested by *eros*. *Agape* is used in ancient texts to denote feelings for one's children or spouse. It can be described as the feeling of being content or holding someone in high regard. *Agape* is the highest form of love there is. This is an unconditional love for others that exists in spite of any character flaws and weaknesses.

————

Love has always been a source of inspiration for poets, songwriters, playwrights, novelists and painters. It is also a dominant theme in music, movies, magazines and TV shows. Through the ages, philosophers and poets from around the world have written more about love than any other subject[71], yet they repeatedly contradict one another when it comes to defining what love means. Some call love "a sickness full of woes" and a "mighty pain", while others assure us that it is a "many-splendored thing" and "the sweetest delight on Earth"[72].

A beautiful Biblical interpretation of love is contained in the words of the famous "Hymn to Love". Found in Chapter 13 of St. Paul's First Letter to the Corinthians[73], it is traditionally read out during Catholic marriage celebrations.

Hymn to Love

Though I speak with the tongues of men and of angels,
but have not love, I have become a sounding brass or a clanging cymbal.

And though I have the gift of prophecy,
and understand all mysteries and all knowledge,
and though I have all faith, so that I could remove mountains,
but have not love, I am nothing.

And though I bestow all my goods to feed the poor,
and though I give my body to be burned,
but have not love, it profits me nothing.

Love suffers long and is kind; love does not envy;
love does not parade itself, is not puffed up;
does not behave rudely, does not seek its own,
is not provoked, thinks no evil;

does not rejoice in iniquity, but rejoices in the truth;
bears all things, believes all things,
hopes all things, endures all things.

Love never fails. But whether there are prophecies, they will fail;
whether there are tongues, they will cease;
whether there is knowledge, it will vanish away.

For we know in part and we prophesy in part.
But when that which is perfect has come, then that which is in part will be
done away.

When I was a child, I spoke as a child, I understood as a child, I thought as
a child; but when I became a man, I put away childish things.

For now we see in a mirror, dimly, but then face to face.
Now I know in part, but then I shall know just as I also am known.

And now abide faith, hope, love, these three; but the greatest of these is love.

The key learning of this masterpiece is that love is the beginning and
the end of everything and nothing matters until you have love.

LOVE AND SCIENCE

Until recently, science did not concern itself with the topic of love.[74] In
1973, in *Colors of Love*, author John Lee identified six basic love theories,
which he termed "colors of love"[75]. Lee compared styles of love to the
color wheel (a circular chart illustrating how different colors relate to

one another). In the same way as there are three primary colors, Lee suggested that there are three primary types of love, loosely based on the Greek interpretations of love described earier. They are: (1) Eros, (2) Ludos, and (3) Storge.

Three primary styles:

1. Eros – Loving an ideal person
2. Ludos – Love as a game
3. Storge – Love as friendship

Continuing this analogy, Lee proposed that in the same way that primary colors can be combined to create complementary colors, these three primary kinds of love could be blended to create secondary types of love. For example, a combination of Eros and Ludos results in Mania, or obsessive love.

Three types of secondary love:

1. Mania (Eros + Ludos) – Obsessive love
2. Pragma (Ludos + Storge) – Realistic and practical love
3. Agape (Eros + Storge) – Selfless love

This theory has been expanded on by Clyde and Susan Hendrick of Texas Tech University. Below are the different love styles they have documented:[76]

Eros – This refers to the love of beauty and is a highly sensual kind of love. Erotic lovers choose one another by intuition or "chemistry". They are more likely to say they fell in love at first sight than people in relationships characterized by other types of love.

Erotic lovers view marriage as an extended honeymoon, and sex as the ultimate aesthetic experience. They tend to address their lovers with pet names such as "sweetheart" or "honey". An Erotic lover can be perceived as a hopeless romantic. Those governed by other love styles may consider erotic lovers to have unrealistic expectations; some may even believe them to be trapped in a fantasy.

41

Examples of Eros can be found in numerous mainstream movies, including: *The Blue Lagoon*, *Return to the Blue Lagoon*, *Pretty Woman*, *Working Girl*, *Girl with a Pearl Earring*, *Star Wars* and *Titanic*.

Ludus – Ludic lovers are players. More interested in the quantity rather than the quality of relationships, they want to have as much fun as possible. Ludic lovers choose their partners by playing the field, and quickly recover from break-ups.

Ludic lovers tend to view marriage as a trap and are the most likely of all love styles to commit infidelity. They may view a child primarily as a living symbol of its parents' fertility or of the virility and masculinity of the father. They regard sex as a conquest or a sport, and they engage in relationships because they see them as a challenge.

Examples of Ludus can be found in movies such as *Dangerous Liaisons* and *Cruel Intentions*.

Storge – Storgic lovers are primarily friends. This type of love develops gradually out of friendship, and can endure beyond the break-up of the relationship.

Storgic lovers choose their mates based on homogamy, and will very often be unable to pinpoint the exact moment that friendship turned to love. Storgic lovers will want their significant other to also be their best friend.

Storgic lovers place a great deal of importance on commitment, respect and understanding, and will strive to avoid committing infidelity in order to preserve the element of trust. Children and marriage are seen as legitimate extensions of their bond, but sex is of lesser importance than in some of the other types of love.

Examples of Storge can be found in movies such as *When Harry Met Sally...*, *Love & Basketball* and *Zack and Miri Make a Porno*.

The researchers also identify the following three types of love:

Pragma – Pragmatic lovers are, above all, practical; they think rationally and realistically about their choice of partner, seeking out a person who has common values, interests and goals.

Pragmatic lovers will carefully weigh the costs and rewards of a relationship and strive to avoid the destructive consequences of infidelity. Pragmatic lovers view sex fundamentally as a reward or a means of procreation, and view marriage and having children as either a liability or an asset.

Examples of Pragma are to be found in numerous books and movies, including *Ordinary People* and *Pride and Prejudice* (Charlotte in particular).

Mania – Manic lovers often have low self-esteem and place a great deal of importance on their relationship.

Manic lovers tend to use possessives and superlatives to describe their partners, and will often say they "need" their partners. Love, for them, is a means of rescue, or a reinforcement of self-esteem.

Manic lovers will avoid committing infidelity if they believe there is even the slightest chance they will be found out. They view marriage as ownership and children as a potential threat – a rival for their lover's affections, a substitute even for sex. Sex therefore serves to reassure them that they have yet to be usurped by their offspring. Not surprisingly, Manic lovers are often anxious or insecure and can be extremely jealous. However, they tend to respond well to therapy and often grow out of this type of love.

Extreme examples of Mania are depicted in movies including *Misery*, *Fatal Attraction*, *Play Misty for Me*, *Swimfan*, *Taxi Driver*, and TV series *The Office*.

Agape – Agapic love is self-sacrificing, all-encompassing love. Agapic lovers are often spiritual or religious people who view their partners as blessings and do all they can to take care of them.

Agapic lovers will remain faithful to their partners to avoid causing them pain. After a break-up, they will often wait patiently for their partner to return, in the hope that they can patch things up. Marriage and children are deemed sacred, and sex is a blessing between the partners. Agapic love believes itself to be unconditional, although lovers in such relationships often do not pay enough attention to their own needs and risk suffering as a result.

Examples of agape can be found in such books and movies as *The Gift of the Magi*, *Odyssey* (Penelope), *The Mission*, *Somewhere in Time*, *Titanic*, *Untamed Heart* and *Forrest Gump*.

The researchers found that relationships in which both partners expressed and felt the same type of love tended to last longer. This is perhaps not surprising, considering that most people seek out partners who are similar to themselves on some level. However, in my opinion, the "right" type of love is the type that is right for you, or, in the words of a recent movie title: *Whatever Works*.

The last love model mentioned, agape, refers to unconditional love. But what is unconditional love and how does it differ from conditional love? Crucially, with conditional love, the love is "earned" on the basis of conscious or unconscious conditions being met by the lover, whereas with unconditional love, that love is given freely to the loved one, independently of anything that person says or does. Conditional love requires some kind of finite exchange, whereas unconditional love is seen as infinite and measureless.[77]

Unfortunately, most of us never experience unconditional love, and this is borne out by soaring divorce rates, a high incidence of alcohol and drug abuse, violence in schools, and overflowing jails in many societies today.[78]

For many of us, misconceptions about unconditional love start to develop in early childhood when we begin to notice, consciously or unconsciously, that when we do "good" things (for example, we are well dressed, quiet and obedient) people show their approval. They might, for example, smile at us or speak in a soft voice, and we may take this to mean they are expressing love. But this might not be the case. Conversely, when we were "bad" we may have observed that all those demonstrations of "love" were suddenly absent. In short, our experiences taught us that love was *conditional*, that we had to *buy* "love" from the people around us with our words and deeds.[79]

It is important that we understand exactly what unconditional love is so that we can know exactly how to express it completely to ourselves and towards others, as well as fully appreciate it when it is offered to us by others. Unconditional love is the ability to accept, respect, and care for yourself and others without any conditions, limitations or reservations attached to that love. Unconditional love is the practice of giving love to others without demanding that they reciprocate. This kind of love is best embodied by the love between a mother and her child.

Unconditional love has less to do with romance, friendship or relationship and more to do with an abundance of love for yourself that flows out from your body and attracts good things and people into your life like a magnet.[80]

Unconditional love of yourself means accepting everything that is you, including all your flaws and weaknesses (see January – Self-Love). This is the basis of unconditional love, because love in its true form cannot be shared or given to someone else until you love and accept yourself first. There are no boundaries or limits on love that is unconditional. You are not trying to control the actions or behaviors of the other person, nor do you impose conditions on your love by restricting that love if they behave, or don't behave, in a certain way. Unconditional love is the ability to want what's best for others for them to be happy, irrespective of your own opinions and biases of them or their behavior. Unconditional love is an overflow of positive energy that comes from the complete love that you have for yourself; so no matter what the other person says or does, it will not affect your level of happiness.[81]

Unconditional love means that you love another person unconditionally, no matter what. It does not mean that you will put up with destructive behavior because you love them unconditionally. Quite the opposite:

you love yourself and you love others, so your decisions will be based on love, not on co-dependency. If, for example, you are in a relationship with an alcoholic who shows signs of love when he is sober but mistreats you when he is drunk, you would most probably encourage him to seek appropriate medical and psychological attention, in order to help him recover from his debilitating addiction. Your behavior, in this instance, would flow from love, and any action based on love is destined to succeed.

THE BENEFITS OF UNCONDITIONAL LOVE[82]

The practice of giving unconditional love to others requires, by its very nature, that you don't expect anything directly in return. By providing unconditional love, you are, however, expressing your faith that good things will be drawn into your life through the law of attraction.

Even though you do not expect anything from loving unconditionally, numerous benefits will arise:

- The act of giving unconditional love to others means the recipients of your love will not fear or reproach you for any of your behavior. On the contrary, such love facilitates open and honest relationships with other people.

- In a more spiritual sense, sharing your love unconditionally with the world sends out positive energy, which will be returned to you in one form or another to create great abundance, wealth, and goodness that you deserve in your own life.

- When you provide unconditional love to others, you are not dependant on others for happiness, but you derive your happiness from within. Your energy radiates to those around you and the world gives back to you in abundance.

- When you give love unconditionally, then you can't ever be angry at anyone. All human minds need congruency of thought and it's simply impossible to hate another person if you have made the conscious decision that you are going to love them unconditionally.

- By giving unconditional love to others, you side-step any tricks, emotional ploys and unfair negotiating tactics because you have consciously chosen to take responsibility for giving them love from your heart, no matter how they behave.[83]

———————

True love, in its broadest sense, does not discriminate. It doesn't say "I love this person, but not that one". It just loves. Unconditional love means loving another person to the extent that you would support them and love them in whatever it is they need to do in order to further their own learning and evolution.[84]

Unconditional love requires not only mental and spiritual practice and study, you must also show your unconditional love for the natural world around you: for the skies and the seas; for the cooling breeze we feel on our heads and shoulders, which ruffles the blades of grass; for the colorful wild flowers nourished by the mountain mist, and the rain that refreshes plants and soil; for the trickling brook, the rocks and animals and the birds that sing. It also requires us to love all people, independent of the color of their skin, their race, religion, sexual preferences, viewpoints or status.[85]

It is no exaggeration to say that our emotional need for unconditional love is just as great as our physical need for air and food.[86]

In fact, "there is so much conflict in the outer world that we see on the television news because there is so much inner conflict within people. The physical world reflects exactly what is going on within the human psyche" (See April – Reality Creation). "The inner turmoil and conflict creates its outer reflection – everything from a family row to muggings, rape, terrorism and war. Conflict will only end in the outer world when we find peace within our inner world – our consciousness. There will be peace and love on Earth when we find peace and love in our hearts. **When we love and respect ourselves, we will create a personal – and together, a collective – reality that will mirror that inner love and harmony as an outer love and harmony.**

All we need to do is change ourselves and everything will flow from that. Heal yourself and you heal the world.''[87]

The consequences of a lack of unconditional love are truly dramatic. If we don't have enough real love in our lives, the resulting emptiness is unbearable. We then compulsively try to fill the emptiness within us with whatever feels good in the moment, be it money, anger, sex, alcohol, drugs, violence, power, or the conditional approval of others. Anything we use as a substitute for real love becomes a form of imitation love, and although this may feel good for a moment, it never lasts and never gives us the feeling of genuine happiness that real love provides.[88]

Most people spend their entire lives trying to fill their emptiness with imitation love, but all they achieve is an ever-deepening frustration, punctuated by brief moments of superficial satisfaction. All the unhappiness in our lives is due to that lack of real love and to the frustration we experience as we desperately and hopelessly try to create happiness from a flawed foundation of imitation love. The beauty of real love is that it will always eliminate our anger, confusion and pain.[89]

As you continue to send out love, the energy returns to you in a regenerating spiral. As love accumulates, it keeps your system in balance and harmony. Love is the tool, and more love is the end product.[90]

Science has now recognized that our so-called reality is in fact based on strings of vibrating particles. In other words, we and everything else in the universe consist, in essence, of vibrations. And the ultimate vibration – the highest, lightest, fastest, finest, largest, most powerful of all frequencies – is unconditional love.[91]

The vibration of unconditional love is sheer joy, utter bliss, total transcendence. It is the healing, uplifting source of all that is. Some of us call that ultimate love vibration "God", others use different names. The moniker makes no difference. God is love. Love is God.[92]

The achievement of unconditional love requires awareness born out of regular practicing of proven and tested spiritual methods such as meditation [93] (See October – Awareness). So try the following exercise to trigger unconditional love within you.

EXERCISE 11: LOVE UNCONDITIONALLY

Make the conscious decision to love unconditionally with a love that does not discriminate.

Bring yourself to a meditative state. Once you are in deep meditation, realize that unconditional love is the source of peace and happiness and that from now on you will be loving unconditionally, and that you are healing the world by unconditionally loving yourself and others.

———

When you begin to love everyone unconditionally, including yourself, the people around you begin to mirror your loving energy. They will then love you and cooperate with you in a way that they never could have done before.[94]

January - Self-Love

You must love yourself before you love another. By accepting yourself and fully being what you are, your simple presence can make others happy.[95]

JANE ROBERTS

Look around you and you'll notice all sorts of different people. There are happy people with a twinkle in their eye; fun to be with, and in love with life and in love with themselves. Then there are the psychic vampires: people who walk into a room and drain all your energy, leaving you feeling gloomy and morose. And that leaves the rest: people who are neither one extreme nor the other but are somewhere in between.

What distinguishes the former group of people from the latter and all those in between? The amount of self-love they have.

By self-love I don't mean narcissism, which suggests all manner of vain, egotistical and selfish traits.[96] Loving yourself means acknowledging that you are a divine being of light, that you are a unique expression of the divine mind, that you are precious and unrepeatable, and that you are incredible, powerful and deserve to be loved by the whole world and by yourself.

How many times have you heard others say that you're not good enough, that you're underachieving, or that you're unworthy? How many times did you agree? P.S. If you admitted to any feelings of inadequacy, then the answer is: too many.

No matter what you've been told all your life, you are the most important person, and the being most worthy of love, in the entire world. So, prepare to get rid of all the thoughts and feelings that have ever flooded into your head and heart that say: "I'm not important, I'm not worthy of love, how selfish would I be to think I'm the most important person in the world?"[97]

Have you ever been loved like you're the being most worthy of love in the whole world? Probably not, and those negative thoughts, and many others, may have been reinforced during your lifetime by people who don't know who you really are. But those thoughts are not yours and now is the time to get rid of them.[98]

EXERCISE 12: I LOVE MYSELF

Look in the mirror. Look at the reflection of this incredible being: a divine expression of unconditional love. This incredible being is YOU. Look in the mirror and say, "I am an amazing, unique being. I am loved by the whole world and this love is unconditional."

Remember: To love oneself is the beginning of a life-long romance.[99]

———————

Do you remember when you were a child? You were happy for no reason. You lived perfectly in the moment. You found magic in everything. Life was a joy. You didn't judge yourself. You thought you were perfect just the way you were.[100] Continue this line of thinking, *know* that you are perfect the way you are – both physically and mentally.

To love yourself is to give yourself permission to live as you choose. To love others is to give them permission to live the way they want.[101]

When you love yourself, you accept yourself as you are at any moment – in all your humanity – with fears, weaknesses, desires, beliefs and aspirations that are all facets of who you are. You do not judge yourself or your actions as right or wrong, but accept every moment as an experience from which you will learn, thereby facing the consequences of your actions and decisions.[102]

Essentially, self-love means having an unshakable sense of belief in everything that makes you who you are – not an arrogant, or vain, conviction that you are better than everyone else, but a healthy respect for yourself and everything you stand for. Loving yourself also means taking care of yourself, because doing so reflects on every action and every interaction in your life, from wearing a warm coat in winter to guard against the cold, to quitting a job you hate. It means taking responsibility for your own wants and needs in exactly the same way that you would expect others to care about you.[103]

Self-love is not always encouraged during our formative years. In fact, most of us need to work at it by the time we are teenagers or young adults. We can all feel inadequate about something. Maybe we may imagine we're not bright enough, or that we're a bit flabby and out of shape. We might also worry that we don't have enough money to pay the bills or go on holiday. Alternatively, our insecurities may manifest themselves in less tangible ways. We may feel socially awkward at times, or spiritually unenlightened. However, we have every right to experience and enjoy self-love and self-respect in our lives, and both are skills that we can learn.[104]

It is by loving yourself that you learn how to love. Love requires knowledge, skills and understanding, and by practicing self-love, you develop the ability to take this love to another level – loving another person.[105]

It is only by learning how to take care of your own emotional needs that you discover how to transmit this love to others. When you respect the integrity of your own thoughts and feelings, you are able to do the same for others.[106]

Self-love is not so much a feeling as it is a lack of self-doubt and self-disapproval. It is about finding the right balance and feeling that you belong as a person. Respect, taking charge of your own life and feeling good are key values. Self-love means that your wellbeing matters to you unconditionally. Here are a few of the characteristics of self-loving people:[107]

- They tend to treat themselves well.
- They see fun and enjoyment as a primary goal most of the time.
- They do not allow themselves to be mistreated by others.
- They are caring towards others — because it feels good to do so, not because they have to.
- They put themselves first. Even those they love are a "close second".
- They find a thought that feels good and put it into practice.

Loving yourself is about treating yourself as you would treat someone who is very precious to you; someone you love so much that you hurt when they hurt, for whom you would move mountains just to see them well and happy.[108]

It can be hard to get the balance right. Putting our loved ones' happiness above our own is not unusual — most of us are prepared to sacrifice our own needs to help those closest to us from time to time. This is particularly true, though not exclusively so, for wives and mothers — but this way of behaving will nearly always backfire on us eventually as it leaves us wanting in some way.[109]

The way this works is similar to the oxygen masks on a plane. In an emergency, you'd need to put one on your own mouth before you could begin to help a fellow passenger. Equally well, you first need to love yourself before you can truly love someone else.

Putting yourself first may sound selfish, but it really isn't. It's not about abandoning everyone else, it's simply about honoring your own wellbeing. After all, how can you truly give all that you are capable of giving if you aren't properly nourished, rested, happy and well? And if you don't love and respect *yourself*, how can you expect others to do the same themselves? So, how can you start loving yourself more?[110]

EXERCISE 13: ACTIVELY LOVING MYSELF[111]

Ask yourself, if you were your own best friend, what gift would you give yourself right now that would make you happier and do you good? Of course, each one of us will give a different answer, but there are certain things that we all need in order to love ourselves:

Take time out to pamper yourself – If you think you don't have time for this, ask yourself whether you'd make time for your best friend if they were in need? Well, you are just as worthy. Book a massage or a facial, or take a stroll in your favorite park – whatever you feel like doing, so long as it's regular quality time dedicated to you.

Get breathless – There is no getting away from it, exercise is crucial for good health and wellbeing. If you don't do any, you are simply storing up problems. It doesn't have to be a sport or the gym; but think "breathless". What can you do that's fun and makes you breathless? Dancing? Walking? Cycling? Doing any of these things for 20 minutes every other day would be a great start.

Rest and sleep – You may think sleep is for lazy, boring people and is just a waste of time? Quite the opposite! When you sleep, your body is busy repairing and healing itself and undoing any damage you may have caused it. Take sleep seriously.

Nourishment – Each time you eat, think of the food as nourishment first, mood enhancement second! Choose healthy food that nourishes you.

Light and air – If you live in a town or city, you've probably noticed how much more alive you feel when you can get away from it all and breathe fresh country, or sea, air. We need sunlight to help us produce vitamin D, which is important for bones and general wellbeing. So spend some time outside every day – you'll sleep better too.

Fun, laughter and play – When was the last time you laughed so hard you almost cried? Or fooled around like a big kid? A good laugh loosens muscles, lowers blood pressure, relieves stress and strengthens your immune system. It feels good because when you laugh, blood is pumped around your heart and lungs, boosting your energy levels. So have some fun and laugh as much as you can!

Confront sources of stress – We all have things in our life that drain us of our energy; things we don't want to deal with because doing so would mean stepping out of our comfort zone. It may be nothing more than a messy desk, but it could be something more emotionally charged, like a feud with a relative. Whatever it is, find a way to tackle it and the energy you'll release

will make your life feel a whole lot better. Nurture, honor and love yourself –
choose only those things that are good for you!

———

The relationship between you and yourself is extremely important as it provides the foundation upon which all your other relationships are built – helping to determine their quality, their depth and their character. In short, it is the working model of how you give and receive love.[112]

The quantity and quality of your self-love is what fundamentally determines how successful your relationships with others will be. If what you seek is an honest, relationship based on love, then you must first learn to love, honor and to value yourself as the most wonderful and lovable being.[113]

You cannot feel true love for others until you feel true love for yourself. What you don't have within, you can't give without. And, because you create your own reality (see April – Reality Creation), if you don't love yourself in that total, unconditional way, you will only attract people who don't love you unconditionally – until you are able to love yourself unconditionally. If you don't love yourself and respect your right to be who you are, how can you expect others to love you for who you are? Self-love is all about freeing yourself from the fear and guilt that is stopping you from being yourself. In turn, true love for others is allowing them to be who they are, even if that differs from what you would like them to be. I love you because you are. I love me because I am. That is love.[114]

My boyfriend and I have been together for over a year. Like any couple, we've had our ups and downs, but overall it's been a happy time for both of us. However, it was only when I truly started loving myself that I felt my partner was opening his heart to me in an affectionate and loving way. Before this moment, I had been behaving in a needy, clingy way – frequently seeking reassurance from him that he loved me and regularly initiating dates and romantic dinners. But everything changed the moment I decided to love myself. I started to make sure I got enough sleep and stopped pestering him all the time to let me stay at his place (and sleeping less as a result). I also began going to the gym regularly (loving my body), rather than putting my boyfriend's needs first all the time and fitting my life around his. All these changes I made in my life had a remarkable effect. Pretty soon, *he* was the one on the phone telling me how much he loved me. And he started to display a side of himself I'd never seen before: cooking romantic meals and popping round to my place just to hug me and tell me he loved me. It was amazing. Loving myself had automatically translated into him manifesting so much more love towards me.

To conclude,

Love yourself first and everything else will fall into line.[115]

LOVE YOUR BODY

Sigmund Freud discovered that the body and psyche are inextricably linked. One of his most famous students, Carl Jung, said, "In the same way that the conscious and unconscious are in constant interaction, the body and the mind are in constant interaction." This statement, more than 50 years old, is affirmed by some of the world's greatest minds. Researchers in this field, such as Wilhelm Reich, John Pierrakos, Fritz Pearls, Louise Hay, have all contributed greatly to our understanding of metaphysical science.[116]

With each illness or disorder, your body is reminding you to love yourself. Through genuine self-love, you allow your heart to guide you to wellness and wholeness.[117]

INCREDIBLE MESSAGES FROM WATER

The Japanese scientist and author Dr Masaru Emoto has conducted a number of experiments, the results of which seem to prove that our thoughts and feelings have an effect on our physical reality. He exposed water to different types of human thoughts, speech and sounds, including music, words and prayer before freezing and examining the resulting crystals using microscopic photography.[118]

Through his research, Dr Emoto has discovered many fascinating differences in the crystalline structures of water from many different sources around the planet. Water from pristine mountain streams and springs formed beautiful, geometric crystalline patterns. Polluted and toxic water from industrial or densely populated areas, however, showed distorted and randomly formed crystalline structures.[119]

Having observed water react differently when exposed to a number of different environmental conditions, Mr Emoto and his colleagues decided to see how untreated, distilled water from a drug store was affected by music. A bottle of water was placed between two speakers and different types of music were played at normal volume.[120] Beethoven's Pastoral Symphony, for example, with its bright and clear tones, resulted in beautiful, well-formed crystals. In fact, all the classical music to which the water was exposed resulted in well-formed crystals with distinctive characteristics. In contrast, the water exposed to aggressive, heavy-metal music resulted in fragmented and malformed crystals.[121]

At a later stage, Dr Emoto wanted to see how water was affected by words. A range of different phrases such as "thank you" and "you make me sick" were written on pieces of paper and wrapped around the bottles of water with the words facing inwards. Water exposed to "thank you" formed beautiful, hexagonal crystals, as in figure 2 but water exposed to the phrase "you make me sick" produced irregular crystalline structures similar to the water exposed to heavy-metal music, as in figure 3.[122]

Figure 2. Thank you[123]

Figure 3. You make me sick[124]

To date, one of the most beautiful crystals created by Dr Emoto's experiments was formed from exposure to the words "love and gratitude". This teaches us that the impact of both love and gratitude on the world can be enormous.[125] When you continually think thoughts of love and gratitude, you simply cannot help but be changed. Such thoughts will change the water within you, which will almost certainly mean a changed you.[126]

After performing experiments on distilled water, Dr Emoto wanted to see what would happen when feelings were communicated to lake water by praying and saying words of thanks to it. Before the experiment, which was conducted at Fujiwara Dam in Japan's Gunma Prefecture, the water did not form crystals. However, after an hour of reciting prayers by the side of the lake, beautiful hexagonical crystals began to form in the liquid.[127]

From Dr Emoto's research it became clear that the way in which water improves or deteriorates is a reflection of the information it has taken in. Clearly, as human beings, we are also affected by the information we absorb because 70 per cent of an adult's body is water. At conception, a fertilized human egg is 96 per cent water. At birth, a baby is 80 per cent water, but as the child matures this figure drops until it stabilizes at about 70 per cent when adulthood is reached.[128]

Because of its high water content, your body is continuously impacted by the vibrations from the negative or positive words you send into it. When you send your body loving thoughts and energy, each cell within it relaxes and takes on a healthier, more powerful configuration. It has also been proven that strong states of self-love boost our body's immune system, allowing us to more effectively fight off invading microorganisms and viruses.[129]

Therefore,

Plant your own garden and decorate your own soul, instead of waiting for someone to bring you flowers.[130]

But words are not just words, they are vibration. Music is not just music, it is vibration. The vibrations we surround ourselves with are the vibrations that will constitute our very essence. We must take special care of what we surround ourselves with, what we listen to, and what we think and feel, as this will determine not only our wellbeing but also that of others.

Since we are made mostly of water, and we have just seen how water reacts to thoughts, we should be showing our body love and appreciation.

There are so many ways to love your body:

EXERCISE 14: QUE LINDA MANITO

In the movie *Paris, je t'aime*, there is a scene when a young mother is singing this Spanish lullaby to her baby, in praise of every part of the child's body.[131] Do the same thing. Make up a song with lyrics that appreciate your body, then sing it to yourself. Love yourself this way!

Qué linda manito que tengo yo, (What a pretty little hand I have,)
qué linda y blanquita que Dios me dio. (What a pretty little white hand God gave me.)
Qué lindos ojitos que tengo yo, (What pretty little eyes I have,)
qué lindos y negritos que Dios me dio. (What pretty little black eyes God gave me.)
Qué linda boquita que tengo yo, (What a pretty little mouth I have,)
qué linda y rojita que Dios me dio. (What a pretty little red mouth God gave me.)
Qué lindas patitas que tengo yo, (What pretty little feet I have,)
qué lindas y gorditas que Dios me dio. (What pretty little chubby feet God gave me.)

EXERCISE 15: WAYS TO LOVE YOUR BODY[132]

- *Think of your body as the vehicle that transports you to your dreams. Honor it. Respect it. Fuel it.*

- Create a list of all the things your body lets you do. Be thankful for it.

- Become aware of what your body can do each day. Remember it is the instrument of your life, not just an ornament.

- Walk with your head held high, supported by pride and confidence in yourself as a person.

- Count your blessings, not your blemishes.

- Be your body's friend and supporter, not its enemy.

- Consider this: your skin naturally replenishes itself once a month, your stomach lining every five days, your liver every six weeks, and your skeleton every three months. Your body is extraordinary – be sure to respect and appreciate it.

- Every morning when you wake up, thank your body for resting and rejuvenating itself so you can enjoy the day.

- Every evening when you go to bed, tell your body how much you appreciate what it has allowed you to do throughout the day.

- Find a method of exercise that you enjoy and do it regularly. Don't exercise to lose weight or to fight your body. Do it to make your body healthy and strong and because it makes you feel good. Exercise for the three Fs: Fun, Fitness, and Friendship.

- Put a sign on each of your mirrors saying, "I'm beautiful inside and out".

- Choose to find the beauty in the world and in yourself.

- Eat when you are hungry. Rest when you are tired. Surround yourself with people who remind you of your inner strength and beauty.

You will see that when you love your body, your body loves you back. By taking care of yourself in as many ways as you can think of, your body will become a strong, healthy and beautiful vessel that will remain your best friend for life.

SELF-LOVE IN MAGIC

Self-love is key to all mental work. When you love yourself, it's easy to improve relationships because you're capable of giving love and allowing others to love you. When you love yourself, you don't need to use food as an anaesthetic to dull the pain of low self-esteem, so maintaining a healthy weight becomes easy. When you love yourself, your vibration is high and you naturally attract money and everything else you desire. As you bask in the magic of self-love, you will find that you truly can have, can do, and can be, whatever you desire![133]

When you activate the habit of letting in deeper feelings of self-acceptance and self-love, the world becomes a truly magical place. By bathing in the vibration of love, you actually experience the entire world from a softer, more empowered perspective. The mundane becomes sacred, and everyone you meet feels deeply connected with the Divine. Indeed, the simplest daily experiences become doorways to the Divine, through which you develop a higher awareness of a natural, effortless connection with your divine essence. This helps you to receive the most loving relationships and enjoy abundant wealth, good health and a highly satisfying career![134]

One of the magical aspects of practicing self-love is that it becomes very easy to manifest anything you want into your life. The vibration of love is the foundation for manifesting the highest levels of success in this material world. When you completely love and accept all aspects of yourself, you send out such a strong energetic vibration into the universe that you become a massive manifesting magnet! You'll find that everyone and everything around you simply wants more of whatever you've got. For them, receiving even the briefest of glances from you can be deeply affecting – flowing as it does from the deep well of self-love within you.[135]

The energy of love physically vibrates at a much higher frequency than any other emotion. Lower vibrational feelings such as fear, greed, need, impatience, or frustration only block you from manifesting everything your heart desires. Through increased levels of self-love you will naturally shift the vibration within your mind-body, transforming yourself into a powerful source of magnetic energy that attracts those divine experiences, relationships, and financial opportunities into your life. The more love you shower onto yourself, the more the universe showers its abundance of every kind onto you.[136]

February – Loving The One / (Finding The One)

We waste time looking for the perfect lover, instead of creating the perfect love.[137]

TOM ROBBINS

Have you ever heard of anybody wanting to be lonely and unloved? I haven't. We all want to love, and to be loved. This is hardly surprising because the source of everything is love; each and every one of us is the fruit of our parents' love.

A lot of my friends are single, but this doesn't mean they don't want to be in a couple. Some may be holding out for "The One". Others might even have found their "other half" at an earlier stage in their life, but have then grown apart. Perhaps they no longer shared the same goals and desires in life.

Clearly, it is far better to be single and independent than to waste your time and energy on the wrong person, but are these scenarios the best we can hope for during the course of our love lives? And are they the only routes to a fulfilling love life?

THE "PERFECT PARTNER"

We all aspire to the "perfect love" and the "perfect partner". But what do these terms mean?

To me, perfect love is synonymous with unconditional love (see January – Love Vibrations, Unconditional Love), while a perfect partner is someone who is perfect for you:

I love you, not because you are perfect, but because you are so perfect for me.

And what is a perfect relationship? This would be a relationship that is perfect for you, but more on that in March – Loving The One 2.

Some of us go to extreme lengths when trying to find the "perfect partner". Some are on a quest to find their ultimate lover; their soul mate; their equal: a person with whom to share their every interest and belief. But having these expectations means you will always be destined for disappointment and will never experience the satisfaction of a loving relationship.[138]

As individuals, we all have a unique set of opinions, philosophies, political beliefs, hobbies, musical tastes and habits, etc. For a relationship to work, it helps if your partner shares at least a few of these, but they shouldn't be expected to share every single one. In fact, some of the differences between you and your potential partner may actually serve to build a stronger, more loving relationship. For example, if you are somewhat hot-headed but your partner has the patience of a saint, he or she will be better at dealing with situations that call for restrained diplomacy. Perhaps your partner is an avid skier, and you have always wanted to try skiing. Well, now is your chance to have a go at something you have always wanted to do. On the other hand, certain differences may cause problems in a relationship. For example, say your potential partner goes on hunting expeditions most weekends, all season long. If you are unhappy about being alone so much of the time on account of his sport and, on top of that, you are morally opposed to hunting, his pastime may well become a source of conflict. It all depends on how tolerant you both are of each other's differences.[139]

We need to look consciously at these differences to decide whether we are right for one another. Relationships may be built on a foundation of love and sexual attraction, but they are cemented in place by compatibility, which, as we have seen, does not necessarily mean sameness.[140]

Instead of seeking the perfect partner, you need to look for a partner who is right for you. Finding the right person is only the beginning, however. Without putting in the work, even the most perfectly matched couple will eventually start to wobble. Many of us learn this the hard way, and come to regret that we didn't work harder at our relationship while we still had the chance. Some of us go from relationship to relationship hoping to find "the perfect one", only to find ourselves missing an ex whom we now recognize, in our heart of hearts, was right for us all along.[141]

Why do we find ourselves hopping from one relationship to another, constantly feeling disappointed by our partner? Answer: expectations.

GREAT EXPECTATIONS

Expectations are the biggest destroyers of relationships and a prime cause of emotional distress. They anchor us mentally and emotionally to a point in the future, never allowing us to enjoy the present. We start by having expectations of what will happen; how a person will behave; what they will do and say. Then, when that person does not turn out the way we expected, we are disappointed. We may lose our temper with them or sulk, or tell our friends how disappointed we are; how he or she was nothing like we expected. But if we'd stopped and thought about it for a second, we would have realized that it's not that person's fault they did not "live up to expectations" – they had no say in what those expectations were going to be, they were just being themselves. The person who created the expectations enabled the subsequent disappointment. But if there were no expectations, there would be no disappointment. Without expectations, we live in the present, not the future, and we enjoy each moment as it happens without destroying that enjoyment with the disappointment of unfulfilled expectations.[142]

Expectations also focus our minds on a very narrow area of potential experience – what we expect the experience to be. Once we let

67

go of expectations, our mind is free from that limited vision and a whole range of possibilities open up. If you enter a relationship with expectations, you are almost certainly going to be disappointed because people are not clones of our expectations of them. If we love someone unconditionally (see December – Love Vibrations, Unconditional Love), without demanding they meet our expectations, the relationship takes on a whole new dimension and becomes much more stable and permanent.[143]

THE "OTHER HALF"

When lovers refer to their partner as their "other half", few realize they are quoting a phrase from one of Plato's most famous works, *The Symposium*. This masterpiece, dating from 385 BC, is written from the viewpoint of Aristophanes, the greatest comic poet in Athens at that time and a brilliant and beloved playwright.[144]

Aristophanes argued the following:[145] *In the first place ... the original human nature was not like the present, but different. The sexes were not two as they are now, but originally three in number; there was man, woman, and the union of the two, having a name corresponding to this double nature, which had once a real existence, but is now lost, and the word 'androgynous' is only preserved as a term of reproach. In the second place, the primeval man was round, his back and sides forming a circle; and he had four hands and four feet, one head with two faces, looking opposite ways, set on a round neck and precisely alike; also four ears, two privy members, and the remainder to correspond. He would walk upright as men now do, backwards or forwards as he pleased, and he could also roll over and over at a great pace, turning on his four hands and four feet, eight in all, like tumblers going over and over with their legs in the air; this was when he wanted to run fast.*

Now the sexes were three; and such as I have described them; because the sun, moon, and earth are three; and the man was originally the child of the sun, the woman of the earth, and the man-woman of the moon, which is made up of sun and earth, and they were all round and moved round and round: like their parents. Terrible was their might and strength, and the thoughts of their hearts were great, and they made an attack upon the gods; of them is told the tale of Otys and Ephialtes who, as Homer says, dared to scale heaven, and who have laid hands upon the gods. Doubt reigned in the celestial councils. Should they kill them and annihilate the race with thunderbolts, as they had done with the giants, then there would be an end of the sacrifices and worships which men offered to them; but, on the other hand, the gods could not suffer their insolence to be unrestrained.

At last, after a good deal of reflection, Zeus discovered a way. He said: 'Methinks I have a plan which will humble their pride and improve their manners; men shall continue to exists, but I will cut them in two and then they will be diminished in strength and increased in numbers; this will have the advantage of making them more profitable to us. They shall walk upright on two legs, and if they continue insolent and will not be quiet, I will split them again and they shall hop about on a single leg.'

He spoke and cut men in two, like a sorb-apple which is halved for pickling, or as you might divide an egg with a hair; and as he cut them one after another, he bade Apollo give the face and the half of the neck a turn in order that the man might contemplate the section of himself: he would thus learn a lesson of humility. Apollo was also bidden to heal their wounds and compose their forms. So he gave them a turn to the face and pulled the skin from the sides all over that which in our language is called belly, like the purses which draw in, and he made one mouth at the center, which he fastened in a knot (the same which is called navel); he also molded the breast and took out most of the wrinkles, much as a shoemaker might smooth leather upon a last; he left a few, however, in the region of the belly and navel, as a memorial of the primeval state.

After the division the two parts of man, each desiring his other half, came together, and throwing their arms about one another, entwined in mutual embraces, longing to grow into one, they were on the point of dying from hunger and self-neglect, because they did not like to do anything apart; and when one of the halves died and the other survived, the survivor sought another mate, man or woman as we call them, and clung to that. They were being destroyed, when Zeus in pity of them invented a new plan: he turned the parts of generation round to the front, for this had not been always their position and they sowed the seed no longer as hitherto like grasshoppers in the ground, but in one another; and after the transposition the male generated in the female in order that by the mutual embraces of man and

69

woman they might breed, and the race might continue; or if man came to man they might be satisfied, and rest, and go their ways to the business of life: so ancient is the desire of one another which is implanted in us, reuniting our original nature, making one of two, and healing the state of man.

Now, tell me you actually believe all of this! As beautiful and romantic as it may sound, I simply cannot accept that we were born to this world incomplete and needy of "the other half" to complete us. Nevertheless, I have met many happy couples who refer to each other as "my other half". Now they have found each other, they feel complete, they say. This absurd sentiment is at the heart of the myth related above. And it is exactly that: a myth. You may need others to assist you in the development of certain areas, but no one can ever complete you because you are already complete (see December – Self-Love). Only when you are happy in yourself can you find happiness with someone else.

LOVE BEFORE FIRST SIGHT

People talk about finding "The One". To me, it's not about finding The One (or rather one of The Ones) but about creating The One. I believe in love *before* first sight. As with everything else in your life, The One is a manifestation of your thoughts and beliefs. If you are not a conscious creator, then your mind is adrift in the mental sea without direction or purpose. However, practicing meditation, affirmation and visualization (see October – Awareness) lets you become a conscious creator, allowing you to manifest in your life whatever it is you desire.

How to do it? One of the basic principles guiding conscious reality creators is:

Be what you want to attract

Like attracts like. Whatever you think of, whatever you believe in, becomes true. Our thoughts are extremely important. If you think all the good men or women are taken, then that's what you will manifest. If you are afraid of living alone, then your mind will focus on this and living on your own will continue to be a source of dread. Whatever you are focused on, you become, and whatever you already are, attracts more of the same. Joy attracts more joy, wealth attracts more wealth, health attracts more health, etc. So be whatever you are looking for.

At some point in your life you may have asked yourself: "Will I ever find my soul mate?" But have you ever stopped to wonder whether *you* are willing to be the perfect soul mate for someone else? If what you want is a long-term relationship, full of passion and love, then all you need to do is find ways to express these emotions to others.

So, it's not at all about love at first sight, it's really about love *before* first sight. You attract your own Prince (or Princess) Charming into your life. You manifest him/her through your thoughts and feelings. The good news is that you alone decide your thoughts and feelings, so choose to concentrate only on what is important to you, and use the power of meditation for manifesting him/her into your life.

EXERCISE 16: MAGIC FOR LOVE – MANIFESTING THE ONE INTO YOUR LIFE

Get yourself into a meditative state using whatever method works best for you. When your mind is peaceful and clear, brainstorm for all the characteristics you are looking for in the partner you desire. Let yourself delve deeply into what you really want, not just what you think is possible. Put all those characteristics on paper, with each one flowing naturally into the next. Think about the things that really matter to you. They can be physical characteristics or personality traits, or both. But remember, the unconscious mind struggles to discern negatives, so be sure to use only positive language when describing them. Then think about the person you have described. Envision them in whatever way you wish. Hear their voice. Feel their touch. Inhale their smell. Imagine yourself doing things with them. This can be anything from waking up beside them, eating a meal together, going for a stroll arm in arm, or having sex with them.[146]

As you attract the partner perfect for you, be aware that this person is not your other half, nor will they complete you; they are an individual in their own right, yet they will come freely to you and will recognize that you are someone special and significant. Believe that this person will manifest in your life within a given period of time. Then thank the universe for taking care of it.[147]

HOW DO I KNOW IF MY PARTNER IS THE ONE OR ONE OF THE ONES?

Once you have brought your partner into your reality, how will you know the new person who has arrived in your life (or was there already but you didn't notice) is The One? I once asked my boss if there was a point during most job interviews when he knew he'd found the right person. He told me that on most occasions he was fairly sure very early on, but a full interview was nonetheless important to be absolutely sure. Relationships are no different – you may feel instantly that the person is right for you but to truly understand if they are The One (or one of The Ones), you need time. You need to experience them, because only through experience can we really learn anything.

During your first experiences with your love candidate, there are certain things to look for. I believe it must *feel* right on a physical and a spiritual level. Your bodies must have a biological spark and there needs to be an intuitive understanding between the two of you – a spiritual spark.

Biological sparks fly when you love each other's touch, when your caresses are arousing yet soothing, and when you both yearn to experience a sexual union. The physical connection you have means sex is an amazing experience, although you also both love just hugging and holding hands.

A spiritual spark means you have an uncanny understanding of one another that transcends your bodily senses. You may know what the other wants without having to ask; you see the world in a similar way and your values, priorities and level of spirituality and intelligence are similar. I cannot, for example, imagine a devout Christian being with an atheist – their beliefs would be too different (unless, of course, they agree to disagree). On the other hand, a girl from a Catholic background who has worked out her own belief system could, for instance, be compatible with a boy from a Muslim background who has also found his own spiritual path, free from cultural constraints or religious dogma. A relationship is possible because they are on the same spiritual wavelength, having both learned to look at and question the world around them.

Spiritual chemistry develops through shared activities such as hobbies, sports and spending quality time together. The more you have in common, the better. But let's say you like dancing, fine dining, foreign travel and romantic comedies. Your partner, on the other hand, is the barfly who never steps foot on the dance floor, thinks fancy restaurants are for snobs and would rather explore the cable channels at home than discover far-flung destinations. What can you possibly ever have in common?

Once you think you've found the partner perfect for you, you could turn to self-help manuals to work out if they are The One. But surely it's better to find out by *experiencing* them. Just go for it. Let go, enjoy them, and then take a mental snapshot to see if this feels right. If it does, carry on. If it's almost right but there's something niggling you that you can't put your finger on, give yourselves another chance. After all, if they're a "maybe" you need time to find out if they could turn into an "Oh, yes!" But it is also important to remember that "good" is the biggest enemy of "the best".

To me "The One" really means "one of The Ones". In other words, the right person for you is the right person for a particular period in your life. It could be your whole life or many lives, but it could equally well be a much shorter period. You manifest the right partner for the appropriate time in your life. During this period, this person is there to help you realize your goal. Once you have learnt your lesson and there is nothing more to be learnt together, you may realize you need to part. Part with love, but part in such a way that you both can benefit. Alternatively, with time, the paths of two people may diverge. This means they have made the most of their relationship; both have grown and learnt a lot, but they must now follow separate paths to continue their evolution. And, since you may need various different stimuli from various different people on your chosen path, you will most likely encounter various Prince/Princess Charmings along the way.

Once you have decided that a person is a good fit with where you are in your life, you might want to consider formalizing the relationship. Let's have a closer look at the institute of marriage.

MARRIAGE?

I have great hopes that we shall love each other all our lives as much as if we had never married at all.[148]

According to Wikipedia, marriage is "a social union or legal contract between individuals that creates kinship. It is an institution in which interpersonal relationships, usually intimate and sexual, are acknowledged in a variety of ways, depending on the culture or demographic. People marry for many reasons, most often including one or more of the following: legal, social, emotional, economical, spiritual, and religious. These might include arranged marriages, family obligations, the legal establishment of a nuclear family unit, the legal protection of children and public declaration of love".[149]

Marriage customs and traditions differ according to religion, but most are arrangements for life. One exception to this norm is marriage within the Wiccan tradition. Unlike the Christian form, where the man and woman are joined together in holy matrimony till "death do us part" (even if they later grow apart and eventually come to loathe one another), the Wiccan "handfasting" ceremony joins man and woman "for so long as love shall last". In other words, when there is no longer love between them, they are free to go their separate ways.[150]

In a union such as this, the couple stays together because the love is lasting, not because they feel obliged to remain together for legal, social or economical reasons. Where the latter is the case, the myth that the marriage is based on love is often allowed to endure because the couple is either unable or unwilling to face up to reality.

Speaking of myths, our heads are full of myths about what a good relationship should look like. Many of these probably stem from Hollywood movies and are linked to expectations (mentioned before) we have about a partner.

Let's look at some of the myths that cause so much frustration among couples striving for the perfect relationship:[151]

MYTH: Relationships are easy

Relationships are not easy! People spend a great deal of time, money and energy studying, training and applying themselves in their professions to become the best they can be. Yet when it comes to relationships, many of us assume they will just happen and take care of themselves with hardly any investment of time or effort on our part.

However, to create a truly rewarding relationship, you need to treat it like a garden. You need to tend to it carefully, spend time in it and water it frequently. The results can be spectacular. You may see it bloom in such a way that it provides you with ongoing joy and happiness.

MYTH: Great relationships don't have conflict

In the early stages of a relationship, it can come as quite a shock the first time you experience conflict. Some couples take this to be a sign that the relationship is doomed, but conflict is a normal and healthy part of all relationships. Think of conflict as growth trying to happen. It is an opportunity to look at your differences and understand a perspective other than your own. It is also a time when you can look at your own values and beliefs, while seeking to understand those of your partner. When conflict is used as an opportunity for you to grow as a couple, it can actually facilitate a greater emotional intimacy.

MYTH: My partner should think the same as me

This myth seems to derive from the joyful, bonding stage that most couples go through at the start of a relationship. But it is based on the fallacy that "if my partner and I are one, then we must think, feel, want and need the same things".

When you consider that most couples at this point are experiencing euphoric feelings for each other, it makes sense that they might think this. But this is a dangerous myth to believe. Instead, it is important to accept that your partner is a separate individual to you with different likes, dislikes, wants, needs and interests.

MYTH: It's good to vent all my feelings in my relationship

This myth is also dangerous because it allows you to think it is acceptable to vent all your feelings and thoughts – positive and negative – at your partner. However, such an approach is potentially destructive and can hasten the end of the relationship.

It is important to consider what, and how, you share with your partner. Think about how you treat your best friend. Should you aspire to be your best and treat your partner in a similar fashion, the rewards can be incredible.

MYTH: Sex has nothing to do with a good relationship

Sex has everything to do with a good relationship!

Think of sex as the melting pot of all your relationship issues. If you are drifting apart as a couple and living parallel lives – perhaps working or raising kids with little spare time to invest in the relationship – forging a lasting sexual connection may be the last thing on your mind.

If you struggle to be open with your partner and express your needs and longings, then it is unlikely you will be open in sex.

Have a look at how you both connect and interact and then see how this relates to your sex life. It may be an illuminating experience.

MYTH: The relationship won't improve until my partner does

In couples therapy, it is common for both partners to blame each other for any problems and to insist it is the other person, not them, who needs to change. But this attitude prevents the relationship from developing and improving.

Rather than focusing on your partner, think about how you can change. **When you change yourself, the relationship changes.**

MYTH: My partner should meet all my needs at all times
This myth relates to the symbiotic nature of romantic love. Just like a baby who bonds with its mother and feels at one with her, we sometimes think that one person should be everything for us and meet all our needs. In the distant past, our ancestors would have had a whole village of people to consult with and to help meet their needs. Today, however, we tend to expect one person to do all this for us.

So many myths, so many expectations, so many people searching for love. All this can be so confusing, but in reality it's all really quite simple.

All too often we search for love without realizing that love is inside us waiting to be released. The right person is just around the corner and yet we fail to see it. Rumi, the Sufi mystic, sums this up perfectly when he says:

Your task is not to seek for love, but merely to seek and find all the barriers within yourself that you have built against it.[152]

All we need to do is love, and live our lives full of love. So many of us build a wall around ourselves as a defense against heartbreak. But what kind of a life does that force us to live? Is it not better to experience love and to break down these barriers than to lead an empty life lacking love? The right person exists for the right moment; there is no need for us to build a wall of indifference around our souls out of fear of getting hurt. We get hurt and then we learn from it, allowing us to move on. When you love with true love, there is nothing that can hold you back.

March – Loving The One 2 (Keeping The One)

Laugh as much as you breathe and love as much as you live.[153]

AUTHOR UNKNOWN

We are complete in ourselves just as we are; there is no need for "the other half" as we already have everything within us. Nevertheless, most of us hope to find a wonderful partner to share our lives with, and once we have found (or rather, created) this amazing being, we strive to make this relationship last.

As well as understanding the type of relationship we are currently in, we need to identify what kind of relationship we would most like to have. The Triangular Theory of Love, described below, illustrates how a relationship can be intimate, passionate, committed, or combine elements of any of these three.

TRIANGULAR THEORY OF LOVE[154]

Developed by psychologist Robert Sternberg, the Triangular Theory of Love argues that love, within the context of a relationship, has three main components:

Intimacy – feelings of closeness, connectedness, and bondedness.
Passion – drives that lead to romance, physical attraction, and sexual consummation.
Commitment – in the short term, the decision to remain with another, and in the long term, shared plans and achievements.

These three components – each represented in figure 4 as a corner of a triangle – interact with each other and with the actions they produce. In turn, they also have an effect on the behavior and the feelings that created them. This generates seven different kinds of love experiences (non-love is not represented). The shape of the triangle will vary according to the type of love it represents – which may change over the course of a relationship – and the bigger the triangle, the greater the love.

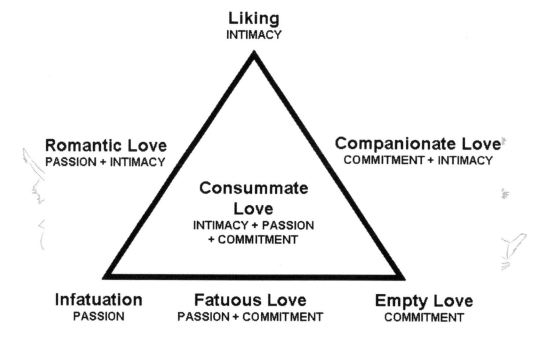

Figure 4. Triangular theory of love[155]

Non-love is the absence of all three of Sternberg's components of love.

Liking. Sternberg says relationships based on liking should not be trivialized simply because they do not involve passion and long-term commitment. Rather, the bonds of intimacy and warmth they generate are the hallmarks of true friendship.

Infatuation is pure passion. Romantic relationships often start out as infatuated love and become romantic love as intimacy builds over time. However, unless commitment also develops, infatuated love may suddenly disappear.

Empty love is characterized by commitment without intimacy or passion. Sometimes, a strong bond of love will deteriorate into empty love. In cultures where arranged marriages are common, relationships often begin as empty love and develop into one of the other forms over time.

Romantic love is forged through intimacy and, physically, through passionate arousal.

Companionate love is an intimate, non-passionate type of love that is stronger than friendship because of the element of long-term commitment. As sexual desire is not an element of companionate love, this type of love is often found in marriages in which the passion has gone but a deep affection and commitment remain. The love shared by members of a functional family is a form of companionate love, as is the love between close platonic friends.

Fatuous love, traditionally exemplified by a whirlwind courtship and marriage, is defined largely by passion without the stabilizing influence of intimacy. This type of love does not, however, describe a relationship in which sex functions to disguise underlying commitment issues or where a partner feels pressurized, or is coerced, into sexual acts. Such relationships tend more towards empty love.

Consummate love is the complete form of love and is the basis for what most of us would recognize as an ideal relationship. Of the seven varieties of love, consummate love is the one most usually associated with the "perfect couple". According to Sternberg, such couples still have great sex 15 years or more into the relationship; cannot imagine themselves capable of happiness with anyone else in the long term; and overcome their few disagreements in a calm, rational way – without losing their dignity. However, Sternberg cautions that maintaining a consummate love can be harder than achieving it in the first place. He stresses the importance of translating the components of love into action. "Without expression," he warns, "even the greatest of loves can die." Thus, consummate love may not be forever. If the passion starts to fade, it risks changing into companionate love.

Who wouldn't want a consummate kind of love? But clearly, if you seek to love in such a complete way, with all three elements included in your relationship, the challenge lies not so much in creating this love (even though this is an achievement in itself) as in maintaining it. When dating, we try to attract a partner by looking our best and being as kind, funny and interesting as we can, in the hope that the other person will fall in love with us. Once in a relationship, these qualities can continue to bond us to our partner, but for this to endure we need to maintain these same types of behavior over time. Of course, what we may ultimately be seeking is the "perfect relationship". But what exactly is this "perfect relationship" we strive for anyway?

PATTERNS OF RELATIONSHIPS[156]

Although most of us think we know what a good relationship entails, we can cause ourselves unnecessary stress by comparing our own relationships unfavorably with ideas about what a relationship should be like. Psychologists who formulate criteria for a "healthy relationship" often fail to understand that few real couples ever achieve this ideal.

There are many different types of relationships, reflecting the wide range of individuals who form couples. Guided by our own relationship history, we tend to choose partners we feel will understand and accommodate our needs, fulfill our expectations and, if we're lucky, help us to address and overcome our fears, enabling us to grow in the directions we need to grow. Recognizing this can enable us to find new ways of discovering and accepting ourselves and our partners.

Most of us will know a couple, or couples, who seem so mismatched that we wonder how they ever got together, and yet despite, or perhaps because of, these apparent differences, have learned to enjoy each other and live together happily. And then there are the couples who seem so devoted to tearing each other apart that we cannot understand how they've managed to stay together. Still others, by contrast, appear to be the perfect pair until we hear they're splitting up or getting a divorce.

Sharpening and deepening our awareness of what we're doing, and how we're doing it, can help us to change our behavior in ways that make a relationship more nourishing and supportive, and less toxic and painful. It can also help us to see what's missing in a relationship and where we're asking the impossible. A clearer perception of our present reality can help us move toward doing a better job of meeting our own (and often the other person's) needs.

Described below are the ten main relationship patterns, all of which can be categorized as either dominant or collateral. It is important to understand how they differ and to recognize which one our current relationship falls into and to decide which one best suits our needs in the long term.

Dominant patterns

1. Survival relationships

These exist where both partners believe they can't make it on their own. Their relationship is not necessarily based on compatibility but is primarily the result of emotional starvation, with each person having concluded before pairing up that almost anybody will do. At its most basic, this relationship embodies the idea that "without you I am nothing; with you I am something". The survival agenda at the heart of this relationship may be physical as well as emotional, including such basic imperatives as finding shelter, getting food and paying the bills.

Since both partners are likely to have few shared interests or complementary qualities, there's little positive "glue" to hold them together when their relationship comes under stress. With each partner trying to get the other to provide what they're lacking, it is likely to be a symbiotic, desperately clinging relationship. Often, it is also subtly or overtly hostile and abusive.

As a result of the desperation for contact and fear of losing it, both partners tend to have a very fuzzy sense of their own personal boundaries. Their contact is characterized by what the psychiatrist Fritz Perls described as "confluence", whereby it is unclear where one person begins and the other ends, and where there is considerable projection of the needs of each onto the other and introjection of the other's definitions of oneself. Each partner is often so out of touch with what they want that they will behave how they imagine their partner wishes them to behave. They may have little tolerance for independence and aloneness and opt to go everywhere together and do everything together. Rather than take responsibility for their own needs, each partner may expect the other to do this for them, with any perceived failure to do so likely to cause offence. The tiniest flicker of independence can be perceived as a threat. For example, if the couple are dining out at a favorite restaurant and one partner orders chocolate cake, this may be perceived as threatening behavior by the other if ice cream has been the dessert of choice for the couple on previous visits. Strong feelings of insecurity tend to play a central role in this type of relationship; the ending of which is usually a sign of growth by one or both partners.

2. Validation relationships

A person may look to his or her partner for validation of their own physical attractiveness, intellect, social status, sexuality, wealth, or some other attribute. Sex and money are especially common validators. For instance, a person in a sexually unsatisfying relationship may choose a new partner for whom sexuality is central: "I was afraid it was me, that I was frigid or something, but my new lover and I have wonderful sex." In such relationships, superficial appearances tend to be valued highly by both partners. For example, physical beauty, expensive clothes, a flashy car, etc.

Since both partners are immature, there is enormous tension and constant testing: "Do you really love me?" A seemingly trivial act or statement can appear highly significant, becoming a source of tears and anguish and overshadowing everything else that the partner has done recently. (This element can also occur in other types of relationships.)

Each partner can be looking for a different kind of validation. For example, a middle-aged professor who takes up with an attractive young female student may want physical and sexual validation, while the student could be seeking intellectual approval.

In such relationships, one partner may continue to require validation while the other starts wanting something deeper. When this happens, both are apt to feel betrayed, empty, and angry. For example, the professor may discover that the beautiful student doesn't give him what he originally thought she would. He grows hungry for real contact, while she may prefer to party with friends her own age instead. In this case, one of the sources of validation they originally had in common has gone. Another example might be the woman who wants security and marries into money, only to discover that even though she's now wealthy she still feels anxious and insecure.

If no deeper basis for connecting materializes and the partners drift apart, there is a strong chance that the needs for validation have been met and the partners have begun seeking something different. At this point, the relationship has done its work. The partners have learned to validate in themselves the qualities they were insecure about and are ready to seek connections in other areas.

3. Scripted relationships

This common pattern is typical among partners who have recently left high school or college. They seem to be the perfect pair, meeting almost all the external criteria for a supposedly ideal relationship. Both partners seek to act out their interpretations of roles they have assimilated over many years. In such relationships, one or both partners will tend to have the "right" kind of job or aspire to be the "right" kind of partner, and they will usually have the "right" kind of house or apartment in the "right" location. Their families will think it's the perfect match. Indeed, such relationships are intended to be for the long haul and are very often child-focused, although ironically, raising children often ends up becoming as much a learning experience for the parents as it is for their offspring.

A variation on this theme is the couple whose main focus is their careers – even if they are parents of young children. In such cases, the partners' families are often still heavily involved on a day-to-day basis, with phone calls or emails to mum and dad being a regular occurrence. Holiday periods are invariably stressful because, without their jobs to distract them, both partners are forced to confront the uncomfortable reality that they struggle with: they realize they cannot please one another, much less the family members who are sure to be involved in some capacity. Because of this, holidays are usually all about obligation and conflict, not relaxation and harmony.

In these relationships, differences often manifest as power struggles. A common source of conflict is how to maintain the illusion of perfection to family and friends; although very often it is not the subject of the argument that is important as much as who "wins". During such rows, any indiscretion or mistake a partner has committed, even if it happened years ago, may be invoked with such indignation that it might seem to an outsider that it had occurred very recently. As well as the ability to talk to each other like mature adults, intimacy and physical attraction are also frequent casualties of this ongoing feud.

In scripted relationships, partners tend to get stuck in long-established patterns and shy away from new experiences. They don't, for instance, discuss the possibility of going somewhere different on holiday or trying out new recipes. Typically, they may divorce in their forties, after 25 years or so of marriage. This often happens because their children who have been the focus of their lives have grown up and left home, leaving them without the shared sense of purpose that has bonded them together. Endings in these relationships tend to be heart-wrenchingly painful and mutually destructive.

However, whether these couples split up or evolve more effective ways of relating to one another is likely to depend on how many points of contact they have. If one partner has an affair, for example, they are likely to split because their method of interacting precludes the possibility of talking about the relationship. When partners begin to relax their tight hold on their scripts and expectations (especially the expectation that "my way is the right way and I wish you'd just recognize it", a scripted relationship may move toward becoming an acceptance relationship or an individuation/assertion relationship, as described below. As these couples start learning to listen, to disclose their deeper feelings, to negotiate, and to compromise, they can provide room for each other to develop and value individual identities. This includes learning to pursue their individual interests and then coming together to share common concerns and pleasures. Partners often find solutions to their conflicts when they begin letting go of entrenched, stereotypical ideas about who has to do what. Perhaps he wants to try a few new recipes out in the kitchen but is all thumbs around the house, while she's handy with tools and tired of cooking and doing the dishes.

Partners in these relationships need to look at all the things they've wanted to do in life but haven't attempted because doing so may have meant challenging the rigid expectations and preconceptions they have of themselves and their partners. They need to learn to communicate at an emotional level, to disclose their feelings and listen to those of their partner. They may need to learn to work less and play more.

4. Acceptance relationships

This is what many of us, including people in the three categories outlined above, typically believe we are getting into when we begin a relationship. In an acceptance relationship, we trust, support and enjoy each other. And within these broad limits, we are ourselves. But each of us also has an idea of which aspects of our personal selves lie outside those limits.

When our expectations are not overwhelming, when the differences between our interests and inclinations are not too dissonant, and when our combative instincts are not too strong, a scripted relationship can evolve into an acceptance relationship. Similarly, when there's enough growth to keep us together and our insecurities allow for honest reassurances, a validation relationship can also grow into an acceptance relationship.

5. Individuation-assertion relationships

These relationships are based on the assertion of each person's wants and needs, and on respect for the other person's process of personal growth. Often they are focused on partners' struggles with what is missing or lacking in terms of self-discovery, becoming whole, and developing their potentialities. They require each person's acknowledgment and appreciation of their differences.

For many couples, this relationship model is the ideal to which they aspire. Although it includes elements of an acceptance relationship, the roles are more flexible and the boundaries more permeable. Partners actively encourage each others' creativity and growth in new directions, and encourage the partner to pursue personal interests with which they themselves have little connection. On a three-week holiday, for example, they may go their separate ways during the first week, then get together for the final two.

Partners in these relationships tend to appreciate differentness, thereby opening up the range of people that they can connect with. Although the partners often look very different on the outside, on the inside their processes for handling conflicts and problems may be similar.

The "working through" process in these relationships demands an ability to tolerate ambiguities. As partners develop goals and resolve problems, they need to have enough flexibility to deal with issues without getting locked in entrenched roles. They need to be open to finding new solutions rather than holding on to some fixed, and often unstated, concept of how things should be done. It's not a major issue when one person wants to try something new. In fact, when this happens, both partners will tend to wait and discover how their feelings evolve rather than act upon preconceived ideas.

For some couples in other forms of relationships, it's easier to move into an acceptance relationship, while for others it's easier to move into an individuation-assertion relationship. In a scripted relationship where partners have very different interests but genuinely care for each other, relaxing the role expectations and creating space for each person to follow his or her own pursuits is one way to step out of chronic power struggles.

The five types of relationships outlined above are the five dominant patterns. There are also collateral patterns, such as healing, experimental, transitional, avoidance and pastime relationships. These patterns tend, by their nature, to be more transient than those described above, lasting from a few weeks (or with pastime relationships, sometime as little as one night) to a few years. When one lasts longer, it is likely to evolve into one of the forms described above.

6. Healing relationships

These liaisons follow periods of loss, struggle, deprivation, stress, or mourning. Typically, one of the partners, or both, will be feeling wounded, fearful and in need of tender loving care, or be seeking to undertake a reassessment of themselves and their ways of relating. Both partners needn't be at the same place at the same time in their own growth and development, and frequently they aren't. Looked at from the outside, the partners may appear to be incompatible. This apparent mismatch could include an age gap of up to 20 or 30 years. There may also be a marked difference in intelligence or sexual attitudes and experience.

Physical distance is common in healing relationships. Couples in these relationships tend to talk about the past a lot, particularly about the struggle or loss that preceded their own relationship. Often they go over and over it, reliving it on different levels as they try to understand and come to terms with it. Gentleness, support and comfort, rather than all-consuming passion, define such relationships. They are also usually play-oriented rather than work-oriented, with plenty of recreation, excursions, and other ways of indulging each other. If the relationship ends rather than evolving into a different form, then both partners will usually grow apart from each other gradually, rather than splitting suddenly and traumatically.

Sometimes, a person may have two or three different healing relationships at once. Also, although most healing relationships are

89

symmetrical, sometimes one person is healing and one is experimenting or transitioning, as described below.

7. Experimental relationships

These are "trying it out" relationships. A man who has always chosen partners emotionally similar to his mother, for example, may decide it's time to try being with someone very different. The intention is to find out how to relate to this new type of person, and what such a relationship is like. This can open a door to finding new ways of interacting with others, and perhaps discovering and nurturing little-known sides of oneself. Dating relationships often have this quality of exploration. When two people in an experimental relationship make a connection that clicks, it may evolve into one of the dominant forms. Similarly, an experimental relationship that almost clicks, but doesn't quite, may influence what a person looks for in his or her next partner.

8. Transitional relationships

These relationships are a cross between the old and the new, between patterns that drove you crazy and others that you were in the process of changing. Such a relationship enables both partners to deal with old issues and conflicts in new ways, but without the trauma of previous relationships. At the same time, it is possible to explore new ways of being and relating. It's a good place to practice for a long-term relationship that's healthier than the one that preceded it, and occasionally it may evolve into one. Take, for instance, the example of a woman whose first husband lied to her constantly – forcing her to rely on her intuitive sense of what was really going on – who becomes involved with a man who was essentially honest but whose love of drama led to exaggeration. In the past, such exaggeration would have enraged her, but now, in a transitional relationship, she allows herself to discover that in the areas that matter most, he is honest.

9. Avoidance relationships

This pattern may involve people who protect themselves against any deep intimacy with others or any full contact with their own deeper feelings. Or it may involve people who have recently left a relationship and who are afraid of yet more of the painful feelings of loss, mourning and failure that often accompany splitting up. Or both. A history of past loss – of a parent, other family member, partner, or close friend by abandonment or death, and the fear that "if I get too close to this person it will happen again" – is a common part of the pattern. The defining quality is that the partners choose someone with whom they can avoid the feelings or patterns of behavior that they want to stay away from.

In some such relationships, the partner may be someone who doesn't easily fit into the other person's day-to-day life. In such instances, there may be a heavy emphasis on sex as a way of suppressing the painful feelings of rejection. Self-disclosure is likely to be low and mistrust (of oneself, the other, or both) high. Often, the beginnings and endings are abrupt.

10. Pastime relationships

A pastime relationship is essentially recreational and is usually recognized by both partners as such. A summer fling is likely to be a pastime relationship. Passionate, delightful and tender while it lasts, there's no expectation that it should be more than that. The dominant mood and theme is "going with it fully for all of what it is".

———

My ideal relationship is the individuation-assertion type. Starting from the belief that we are complete beings, evolving on a path of various lifetimes, this is what I would wish all of you to be part of. But then again, we all need to learn, grow and experience and I don't think we can learn from anyone's mistakes other than our own. So let's just live our love lives at a pace and in a way that feels right.

HOW TO KEEP THEM

There is a sea of literature informing you how to keep a guy or girl, but I will describe this from my own perspective. There are certain things that I have experienced that I highly recommend. They are, of course, based on the assumption that what you want is an individuation-assertion type of relationship:

1. Independent you

As a couple, although your love can be immense, you are not one blended being but two individuals. As two separate people, similar though you may be, you will probably have different needs for alone time. When you were dating, you may have led your own separate lives but regularly spent quality time together. One of the steps to a successful relationship is to continue down this path. Most of us have jobs or school to occupy us, which means we spend much of the time without our partner anyway. The thing is not to start feeling incomplete when your beloved is not with you.

Your lover is the cherry on the cake, not the cake itself.[157]

Let them be; allow them to be free to lead their life and you'll see how they will long to spend time with you and to make this time of the highest quality. Never take your partner for granted and never let them take you for granted. Be a mystery, be interesting, be exciting and be and act complete. When your lover sees that you don't need them and the only reason you would want to spend time together is for pure joy and pleasure, they will become an exciting and excited partner. They will then long for intimacy and become more and more committed.

2. You have an exciting life of your own

Not only are you independent, you also have an amazing life of your own. You have your job, your friends, your interests and hobbies. You are not waiting for anybody to complete you as you are complete by yourself. Your having an exciting life drives your partner so much closer to you. When you know your life is great, they will know it too and will increasingly want to be part of it.

3. You are yourself

Your partner fell in love with you, and, as Dr Suess says:

There is no one alive who is youer than you.[158]

So continue with that. Never change your core to please someone else. If your partner is demanding a profound change from you, it means they didn't fall in love with the true you anyway. Be true to yourself and be yourself, otherwise you are just lying to yourself and your partner.

4. No ghosts from the past

We all have a past, and through this past we became who we are today. But we should acknowledge it, learn from it and then turn the page. When you enter a new relationship, you open a new chapter. You don't want to risk spoiling it by introducing a third person into it, especially when they are from the past and no longer a part of your life. You might still be emotionally attached to an ex partner, in which case you need to resolve this issue. Learn to detach from the past. Enjoy the NOW.

EXERCISE 17: CUTTING THE TIES

Sometimes the bonds we had with an ex may be so strong that they are not easily broken. We become so consumed by memories that we leave no room for the creation of a new, exciting relationship. This is when we can choose to cut the ties with the past. By doing so, the part of the former relationship that has become a burden will no longer be a part of your everyday reality.

Get yourself into a meditative state. Focus on the person you wish to cut your ties with. Imagine you are linked to this individual by invisible bonds of energy. Now imagine you have scissors or a knife in your hand and cut these ties. Push any remaining energy the other person is exerting back to them and draw any of your remaining energy back towards yourself. Leave nothing in between. Let the person go in peace. Wish them all the best and give thanks to the universe for the new reality that has just been created on both sides.

5. You are perfect, almost, and so is your partner

There will always be some small flaws that you could point out in your partner, but that works both ways, so don't do it – at least, not too often. You might even discover that their drawbacks are actually quite cute! Alternatively, they may end up doing something about them. If it's not something that is against your core belief system or priority number one on your "Prince/Princess Charming Characteristics" wish list, then just let it go. Don't forget, everybody has something annoying about them, even the perfect guy/girl – he/she is too perfect!

"There are always core differences between two people, no matter how good or close you are, and if the relationship is going right those differences surface. The issue then is to identify the differences and negotiate them so that they don't distance you or kill the relationship."[159]

It's really all about your vibration. When you feel great about yourself; when you feel happy, powerful and complete, you will send this message to the universe and you will be perceived this way by those around you, your partner included. As such a joyful and powerful being, you will automatically be desirable and attractive and the result will be outstanding – you will draw equally happy and powerful beings to yourself. Be what you want to attract. The law of vibration is always at work and has never failed (see April – Reality Creation).

When talking about relationships, we cannot omit their fundamental component: sex.

SEX

"There is nothing more bonding than cosmic sex. Sex in its highest expression is an ultimate spiritual experience between two people in the dense physical world. It is a means through which we can connect with the highest levels of ourselves and access fantastic creative power. Yet, nothing has been more manipulated and twisted than sex by tabloid papers, religion and pornography. Religion, particularly Christianity, Judaism and Islam, has turned sex into a focus for an explosion of guilt of galactic proportions. While the church parrots the clichés about the world needing more love, the moment you express that love physically for another person outside an institutionalized relationship, it suddenly becomes a terrible sin. Sex – cosmic sex – can take us to soaring into the spiritual realms of being. When partners merge into a male-female wholeness, it raises their collective consciousness to vibratory levels which connect them with higher states of consciousness – oneness. Sex at that level of awareness takes us into timelessness when we are without thought, fear, guilt or resentment. We are out of our bodies and into our deeper self, out of our heads and into our feelings, our spirit."[160]

Since sex is such a powerful phenomenon, we will be blessed if we can incorporate it into our mental works.

EXERCISE 18: SEX MAGIC

This is one of the most powerful forms of magic, for here we are dealing very much with the life forces. Dr John Mumford, in "Sexual Occultism", states that the most important psycho-physiological event in the life of a human is the orgasm. Sex magic is the art of using the orgasm – indeed, the whole sexual experience – for magical purposes.[161]

Just before you start your love-making session, get yourself into a meditative state and focus on what the objective of your work will be. You can involve your partner in this process for increased impact or you can perform this exercise exclusively in your own mind. As you get more passionate, visualize your goal more and more clearly to finally feel it accomplished the moment you explode in climax.

––––––––

As you have seen, there are different types of love, different types of relationships, different ways to make them work. There is no "perfect relationship", just as there is no "perfect partner" in absolute terms. There is only the right relationship for the right moment, and the right partner for the right moment. Let's make our relationships truly magical by appreciating them for what they are on our path of self-growth.

Let us *work like we don't need the money, dance like no one's watching and love like we've never been hurt.*[162]

April – Reality Creation

Reality is merely an illusion, albeit a very persistent one.[163]

ALBERT EINSTEIN

THE SEVEN HERMETIC PRINCIPLES:

Hermeticism is an ancient philosophy that seeks to explain the workings of the natural and supernatural. Its teachings are recorded in written texts that have been passed from generation to generation.[164]

The Seven Hermetic Principles, upon which the hermetic philosophy is based, are:[165]

1. The Principle of Mentalism
2. The Principle of Correspondence
3. The Principle of Vibration
4. The Principle of Polarity
5. The Principle of Rhythm
6. The Principle of Cause and Effect
7. The Principle of Gender

Let's analyze these principles one by one.

1. The Principle of Mentalism

Just as our image in the mirror is a reflection of our body, so the universe and all it contains is a mere illusion, a reflection of the all – our collective mind. The ancient Hermetists used the word "meditation" to describe the process whereby the universe is created in the mind of the all – divine attention – the word "attention" here derives from the Latin root meaning "to reach or stretch out". The act of divine attention is therefore an expansion of mental energy.[166]

2. The Principle of Correspondence

"As above, so below; as below, so above". This principle embodies the truth that there is always a correspondence between the laws and phenomena of the various planes of being and life. There are planes beyond our knowing, but when we apply the Principle of Correspondence to them we are able to understand much that would otherwise be beyond our comprehension. Just as knowledge of the principles of geometry enables astronomers on Earth to map far-off planets, so knowledge of the Principle of Correspondence enables us to extrapolate knowledge of the unknown from the known.[167]

3. The Principle of Vibration

"Nothing rests; everything moves; everything vibrates". This principle explains that the difference between manifestations of matter, energy, mind, and even spirit, results largely from different rates of vibration. An understanding of this principle enables us to control our mental vibrations as well as those of others.[168]

4. The Principle of Polarity

According to this principle, there are two opposite sides – or poles – to everything and everyone, with an infinite number of degrees in between. Of course, judging where one pole begins and another ends is tricky because they are entirely subjective concepts. Try looking at your thermometer and working out where "hot" ends and "cold" begins! An understanding of this principle enables you to change your own polarity, as well as that of others – providing you are prepared to devote the necessary time to studying and mastering this art.[169]

5. The Principle of Rhythm

This principle explains how everything is constantly moving to and fro in a pendulum-like way. Like the oceans, there is a tide-like ebb and flow, with a corresponding high tide and low tide, in accordance with the Principle of Polarity. There is always an action and a reaction; an advance and a retreat; a rising and a falling. Having grasped this principle, you can learn to overcome its effects by applying the Mental Law of Neutralization. Although this won't stop the Principle of Rhythm from taking effect, it will allow you to escape its influence upon you to a certain degree, depending upon how well you learn to master the principle. By doing so, you can learn how to use it, instead of being used *by* it.[170]

6. The Principle of Cause and Effect

This principle explains that there is an underlying reason for every event and that nothing can ever happen by chance. By studying and mastering this principle it is possible to rise above the ordinary plane of cause and effect and to become a causer, instead of an effect.[171]

7. The Principle of Gender

Everything contains masculine and feminine principles. On the physical plane, the principle manifests as sex; on the mental and spiritual planes it takes higher form. No creation – physical, mental or spiritual – is possible without this principle.[172]

Having acquainted yourself with the Seven Hermetic Principles, you now need to familiarize yourself with the Seven States of Matter, something which is essential if you are to understand reality creation.

THE SEVEN STATES OF MATTER[173]

At school, we are taught about the first three states of matter: solid, liquid, and gas. The other sates are less well-known. **The fourth state**, above gas, is plasma, from which stars and fire are made. Plasma is ionized gas, superheated to the point where some of its electrons break away from their nuclei and join other nuclei. Being in an unstable state, the gas molecules behave in a haphazard and unpredictable manner.

99

The fifth state of matter, after plasma, is beam. This differs from the preceding four states in that it is non-thermal. Its particles move harmoniously in one direction, rather than bouncing around randomly and colliding, generating heat.

The sixth state – called the zero state of matter – which is much lower on the scale than any of the previously mentioned five, is the most condensed condensate of all matter. This state of matter was first predicted by the scientist Satyendra Bose. He shared his findings with Einstein, who was so impressed he helped translate and publish them. Their joint venture resulted in the newly discovered state of matter, known as the Bose-Einstein Condensate (BEC).

A BEC exists when matter is frozen to extremely low temperatures – a fraction of a degree above absolute zero. In this state, the atoms overlap to form a wave. The BEC is, therefore, a matter wave. If the wave was compressed, it would form a singularity. If enough mass was condensed into the singularity, it could turn into a black hole.

The zero state of matter, like the fifth state, is also non-thermal: it does not emit heat because its particles are not in motion and so cannot cause friction.

The final state of matter – **the seventh** – is by far the most ethereal concept. It is the thought wave state of matter. Thought wave exists at a higher energetic level than beam and can move even faster – at infinite speed. It is therefore simultaneously "here" and "there", i.e. local and nonlocal.

We live in a mental universe. All matter is a different manifestation of thought wave or etheric matter. All other states are condensations of the highest state.

A further confirmation of the impact of our thoughts on our reality can be found in the famous double slit experiment.

THE DOUBLE SLIT EXPERIMENT[174]

The double slit experiment is one of the most famous physics experiments of all time. It was well illustrated in the 2004 movie *What The Bleep Do We Know!?* You can also find a short clip depicting this experiment on the internet by searching for "Dr Quantum – Double Slit Experiment". Watching this will help you to grasp the principles being demonstrated.

Here's the experiment: We point a laser at a plate with two slits in it. The light goes through the slits and hits a screen at the back. This results in what's known as an interference pattern – several vertical bars. One might ask why are there so many bars. Shouldn't there only be two bars, one for each slit? To understand why the interference pattern appears, we have to understand two properties of waves.

Two properties of waves

The first important wave property is diffraction, which allows waves to move around obstacles. When you shout out, "Dinner time!" the whole family can hear you regardless of whether you have a direct line of sight to them. This is because sound can travel around corners, through doorways, and into people's ears. Whenever a wave goes through a doorway or a slit, the wave spreads out in all directions on the other side. Diffracted waves behave very differently to diffracted particles. When we fire a particle through a slit, it follows a very narrow path on the other side – the smaller the slit, the narrower the path. But when we fire a wave through a slit, it spreads out in all directions on the other side – the smaller the slit, the more it will spread out. So when we shoot light through a slit, it's not going to just make a single spot on the screen, but will go in all directions.

The second important property of light is interference. If two identical waves go through each other, then their intersection will look like the sum of the two waves. Remember, all waves are fluctuations in something. A typical wave alternates rapidly between an upward and a downward fluctuation. If two intersecting waves both happen to be fluctuating upward, then that movement will have twice the amplitude. This is called constructive interference. Conversely, waves moving in opposite directions will cancel each other out. This is called destructive interference.

Return to the double slit experiment

Now that we have an idea of how waves behave, we can forecast the results of the double slit experiment. Some of the light will pass through one slit, and some through the other slit. After passing through the slit, the light will spread out in all directions. The light that passed through the first slit will interfere with the light that went through the other. It interferes constructively whenever both waves fluctuate up in the same place and time and destructively when the waves are fluctuating in opposite directions at the same time. As a result, we only see the spots of an interference pattern where the light interferes constructively.

The particle properties emerge

We might reasonably conclude that a visible interference pattern is proof light is a wave. But what if we were also able to prove that light is a particle? After all, Einstein demonstrated that light comes in tiny individual packets, called photons. What happens if we send one photon through the double slit? According to our previous analysis, the interference pattern requires that at least one wave goes through each slit at the same time for an interference to occur. But if we just have one photon, it can only pass through one slit and hit just one spot on the screen behind.

But when this experiment is performed, the interference pattern does appear. Each photon, of course, hits only one random spot on the screen. But if we shoot, one by one, a series of photons, then the sum of their landing points forms an interference pattern. That is, a photon is much more likely to land in a spot where there is constructive interference. The only way this can happen is if the photon is traveling through both slits at once and interfering with itself!

The conclusion is that light shares properties with particles and waves. Which of the two is it? Neither, of course.

The measurement problem

So, when we shoot a photon through a double slit, it creates an interference pattern. This pattern is only possible if some wave-like behavior is occurring, and if the wave goes through both slits simultaneously. And yet, when we watch where the photon hits the screen behind the double slits, the photon will always land in exactly one spot. Therefore, a photon has some properties of a wave, and some properties of a particle. It is worth adding that the same experiment works with any kind of particle, not just photons. In fact, all particles have both particle-like and wave-like properties.

You may have wondered why this experiment must provide such indirect evidence. If we only need to show that the photon goes through both slits at once, couldn't we just put a measuring device on both slits? Yes, we could. But when we do so, we find that the photon goes through just one slit every time. Furthermore, the interference pattern on the wall disappears! It seems that when we try to gather more observations, the results change!

The Copenhagen interpretation

According to this interpretation, particles can be described by their wavefunctions. Wavefunctions behave like waves. They propagate around walls, and can go through multiple slits simultaneously. They can diffract and interfere with themselves.

Unlike normal waves, we cannot observe wavefunctions directly. If we try to observe a wavefunction, something called "wavefunction collapse" occurs. When a wavefunction collapses, it suddenly becomes like a particle. It appears in exactly one location. If the wavefunction was originally spread out over a large area, the particle will appear randomly somewhere within this area. The probability that it will appear at any given location is based on the magnitude of the wavefunction at that location.

Let's apply the Copenhagen interpretation to the double slit experiment. First, we fire a photon through the slits. At first, the photon is a wavefunction, and thus can go through both slits at once. The wavefunction diffracts, and interferes with itself, creating an interference pattern. But then the photon suddenly hits the screen, and collapses its wavefunction in a random location. Because of the wavefunction's original interference pattern, the photon is more likely to appear in some places than others. If we repeat the experiment many times, we can get a good idea of how the original wavefunction was shaped. And that's how we show that there was indeed an interference pattern.

If we put detectors on the slits, then these detectors will collapse the photon's wavefunction. The photon will become particle-like as it goes through just one of the slits. On the other side of the slits, the photon will spread out its wavefunction again, but since it has gone through only one slit, there is no opportunity for an interference pattern to form. If we repeat the experiment many times, we would find no interference pattern.

Observations and observers

According to the Copenhagen interpretation, wavefunction collapse occurs when a particle is observed. But what constitutes an observation, and who is observing it? The observer does not even have to be a conscious human. If we performed the double slit experiment with detectors on the slits, no interference pattern appears. This remains true whether or not we actually look at the data from the detectors. So, do the detectors themselves count as observers? Further complicating matters are the experiments of quantum erasure, whereby it's possible to set up detectors so that the information they receive is erased after it has been measured. If the information is erased carefully enough, the interference pattern reappears. So, sometimes a detector counts as an observer, and sometimes it doesn't?

At this point, we should clear up a common misconception about wavefunction collapse. Some people confuse wavefunction collapse with observer effect. Observer effect occurs because in order to observe the particle, we must knock it with another particle. Because we hit the particle, when we measure it we find we have changed it. However, this is not the same as wavefunction collapse. There are, in fact, other ways to observe a particle without knocking it with another particle. Wavefunction collapse can occur whether you physically touch the particle or not. We should also add that the observer in no way "decides" where the particle will appear. Wavefunction collapse is entirely random.

It does not matter whether we consider the detectors to be observers or not. Further research has developed a mechanism called "quantum decoherence". In a complicated system, wavefunctions become "decoherent", and no recognizable interference patterns can occur. Any such system will act like an observer and appear to be able to collapse wavefunctions. This is the idea behind the Many Worlds interpretation – an alternative to the Copenhagen interpretation. According to this interpretation, wavefunctions never actually collapse, but only appear to collapse through the mechanism of decoherence. **The Many Worlds interpretation implies that our universe's wavefunction is equal to the sum of many non-interacting, parallel worlds. In other words, all quantum possibilities are realities in a parallel universe.** The advantage of this interpretation is that there are no awkward distinctions between observers and non-observers.

The Many Worlds Interpretation proves that the life we desire already exists in the universe – it is a distinct scenario in the sea of quantum possibility. Now all we have to do is make it happen, and by now we know how to make it happen because we are conscious creators of our reality.

WE ARE WHAT WE THINK

The world we have created is a product of our thinking; it cannot be changed without changing our thinking.[175]

Scientific research in the metaphysical field has demonstrated that we are what we think, that we become what we think, and that what we think in the present, determines what we become in the future. Also, since we can change our thought for the better along any line, we can therefore completely change ourselves along any line.

We may think we are great, but as long as we continue to think small thoughts, we will continue to be small. We become great when we think great thoughts, and to think great thoughts, we must transcend all limitations and mentally enter into the world of the great. We must live in the life of greatness, breathe the spirit of greatness, and feel the very soul of greatness. Then and only then will we think great thoughts. And the mind that continues to think great thoughts will continue to grow in greatness.[176]

Having learnt that the physical body is completely renewed every eight to ten months, you may assume that you are young, but to simply think you are young will not cause the body to look as young as it really is. To retain your youth, you must remove those subconscious tendencies and conditions that produce old age, and you must eliminate worry. You must think thoughts that produce, retain and perpetuate youth. If you wish to look young, your mind must feel young.[177]

To produce health, thought must be healthy and wholesome. It must contain the quality of health and the very life of health. You must dispose of any discord, confusion, worry, fear and other wrong states of mind. Any disease is in fact *dis-ease*, because all illnesses derive from the mind and the body simply manifests the state of mind. If you think wholesome thoughts, and wholesome thoughts only, you will become healthful and wholesome. Such thoughts will have the power to produce health, and thoughts never fail to do what they have the power to do. Place in action the necessary subconscious thought and the expected results will invariably follow.[178]

To apply the full constructive power of thought, you should put into effect the principle that "she can who thinks she can", and you should act in the full conviction that whatever you think you can do, you *can* do, because there is no limit to the power that such thinking can bring forth.[179]

Some of the main reasons why so many of us fail to get what we want in life is because we do not definitely know what we want, or because we change our wants almost every day.[180]

––––––––––

When exploring reality creation we must inevitably mention the Law of Attraction.

THE LAW OF ATTRACTION

Just as electrons are called together in the invisible aether to form an atom, so atoms are brought together by vibrating at different rates of speed to create form. In this way, guided by the Law of Attraction, matter is built up into all the beautiful forms we see.[181]

Like creates like and like attracts like. Thoughts are things. Thoughts are forces. They have form, quality, substance and power. Through your thought forces, you have creative power. What you see with your eyes is only the effect of greater causes that are invisible. Everything exists in the unseen before it is manifested in the seen. The unseen things are cause, the seen things are effect.[182]

Thoughts are entities, things, forces; they are vital, subtle powers. They, like everything else, and every other force in the universe, are subject to law. This law is the Law of Attraction.[183]

Whatever thoughts you think will attract to you thoughts of a similar nature. Just as you create good or bad thoughts, so you determine whether your life will turn out great or awful. If you think a good thought and dwell upon it and nourish it with your meditations, it will not only bless and enrich your life, it will attract hosts of other thoughts of equal power and beauty, which will help you. Therefore, if you think "success" thoughts and affirm them, and cling to them through thick and thin, you will attract such a wave of powerful, constructive and inspiring thoughts that you will transcend your problems and be carried, as if by invisible forces, along the path of accomplishment.[184]

On the other hand, it is equally true that if you think a weak, low, vile thought or a thought of failure, you will attract a host of similar thoughts, which, by their very nature will make your life unpleasant and unrewarding.[185]

Think "success" and thousands of invisible forces will fly to your aid. Think "failure" and innumerable forces will help to compound your failure. If thought is the greatest power of all powers, the most vital, subtle and irresistible force in the universe, and if your thoughts have the power to attract other thoughts of a like character, then the choice of your thoughts is the most important act of your life. By choosing your thoughts you choose success or failure, happiness or misery, health or disease, hope or despair.[186]

By the use of carefully graded affirmations, we break the power of evil thought habit, and in its place create a new mental attitude that is hopeful, strong, cheerful, successful; an attitude of mind that knows no failure, can never be discouraged, that stands firm and unafraid amid the changing scenes of life; an attitude of mind that overcomes, conquers and achieves; an attitude of mind that lives in a sea of positive, helpful, stimulating thoughts that are the products of the best minds of all ages.[187]

Using affirmations (see October – Awareness), we can direct our thought stream into the right channel; using affirmations, we can impress upon our mind thoughts, which when translated into actions, lead to success and accomplishment. Through affirmations, we can learn to break the invidious cycle of bad habits, and in its place develop habits that make our lives rich and rewarding. Through affirmations, we can build up our characters, changing what was once weak and insecure into something powerful and stable. Through affirmations, we can concentrate our consciousness upon thoughts of power, success and courage and these, in turn, will attract to us multitudes of other thoughts of a similar nature. Do you realize, dear reality creator, the extent of the wonderful power that you possess?[188]

EXERCISE 19: CREATE YOUR OWN REALITY

The key learning of this chapter is that:

You create your own reality.

Make affirmations to suit your particular needs. Whatever you desire to do, affirm beforehand that you can do it, and that you will do it. Whatever seemingly disagreeable and difficult effort lies before you, deny failure and affirm beforehand that you can and will do it, and that already in your mental world it is accomplished. Then visualize yourself doing this thing calmly and without effort. Know that you will succeed.[189]

What would you be doing if all your desires were already manifested? You would be enjoying them, indulging in them, feeling powerful and grateful for what you have created. You would be completely happy and joyful. This is exactly the state that puts us in alignment with the manifestation of our desires. When we feel our dreams have already come true, we are in vibrational harmony with their manifestation. In manifesting, we begin by experiencing the end result. On a mental plane, our creation already exists and it only takes time, concentration and belief to have it manifest on a physical plane.

May – Energy, Auras & Chakras

You don't create through action, you create through vibration. And then your vibration calls action from you.[190]

ABRAHAM-HICKS

Everything around you in the material world that you can see and touch – houses, people, animals, cars, food, etc. – is made up of energy bound together to form matter. So in essence, we are all living, breathing energy units. And because energy is vibration, our lives can be seen as a symphony of vibrations, with each one of us pulsing at our own unique frequency.[191]

Everything that is visible in the physical world must first be formulated on the etheric level. From here, it passes to the thought level and then to the mental level, before manifesting in the material world that we live in (see April – Reality Creation).[192]

This transition is the springboard for all creative acts – whether you are an artist, a cook, or a gardener – and can be compared to developing a photographic image. You cannot have a perfectly composed, high-resolution photograph without first producing the perfect negative. Equally well, it is impossible to achieve your goals in the physical realm until the blueprint for your actions has first been conceived on the mental plane, in our thought world. The more clearly you visualize this, the better its chances are of manifesting in the physical world. But crucially, this should be what *you* really want and not what others want for you – or what you think you should want.[193] The blueprint you are creating in your mental plane must have a joyous, emotional component because it is the feeling of excitement and happiness that you experience during your mental creation that ensures the perfect end result in the physical world.

Energy is vibration. It is the starting point of reality creation, and the vibration of your thoughts and feelings radiates out into the world from your every pore. If you think negatively, then your vibration will be low. Accordingly, your aura will be colored with this negativity and this will be felt by everyone you come into contact with. Furthermore, according to the Law of Attraction (see April – Reality Creation), the type of energy you emit will be the type of energy you attract.[194]

With knowledge of energy vibrations, you can learn to control your own vibration, enabling you to take charge of everything that affects you. This is because your vibration and everyone else's are connected. Unfortunately, most of us assume the only way to change what we don't like in our life is to gain control of the people, the events and the circumstances surrounding us. But this is impossible, and only serves to feed our feelings of frustration and vulnerability. What we should instead be seeking to control is our vibration.[195]

Everything around you is vibrating, and when you turn your attention to something and maintain that focus, you begin to include its vibration in your vibration. Therefore, when you see something you want and you apply your thoughts to it, and say yes to it, you are incorporating its vibration into yours. Equally well, when you see something you do not want, and you shout no at it, you integrate its vibration with yours. In this vibrational world, we communicate far more with other people through vibration than we do by talking.[196]

Think of yourself as an energy system. Everything inside you is connected and intelligent. Whatever you see manifested in your physical body – be it health or illness – has it's origin in your energetic body. To fully understand this interconnection we need to be familiar with the concept of auras and charkas.

AURAS

In metaphysics, the aura is an emanation from the soul of the person whom it surrounds. Similar to the rays of the sun, or the fragrance of the flower, it is an energy field made up of varying types of live and intelligent vibrations or frequencies. The human aura is egg-shaped and extends to a distance of between a half and one meter from the body of the person emanating it.[197]

The human aura is composed of various elements, some of a low and some of a high order, corresponding to the elements manifesting in the soul of the person. Just as the manifestation of the souls of different people varies greatly, so too do their auras. And in the same way we glean information by glancing at the pages of a book, an advanced occultist, with trained clairvoyant vision, is able to ascertain the mental and emotional character of a person simply by observing the appearance and the color of his or her aura.[198]

The lowest element in the human aura is that which occultists call the "physical emanation". It is almost colorless except for tiny, thin "streaks" that protrude from the body like bristles on a brush. When a person is in good health, these "bristles" stand out stiffly, but when they are ill or suffering from impaired vitality, they droop like the petals of a wilted flower. When we move around, minute particles of this element of the aura appear to become detached. It is thought these particles are the essence of the so-called "scent" that dogs and other animals follow when they track us.[199] I believe this is also what makes us perceive certain places as friendly or hostile. We can easily feel the auric influence of the people who have been in a certain place before us. This feeling tells us if the place we are in is filled with love or with suffering. When my brother first saw my new flat he said something like: "There is a good atmosphere here, it feels good." This makes sense to me because the apartment is filled with love, spiritual growth and fun.

Passing over several unimportant auric elements of a lower degree, let us consider the most interesting phenomena of the auric colors: those that represent the mental and emotional elements of the soul. These elements are the characteristic features of the aura when perceived by clairvoyant vision. The aura, seen in this way, presents the appearance of a luminous cloud composed of varied and shifting colors, gradually growing fainter toward its outward limits until they finally disappear.[200]

Each one of these auric colors represents a particular thought, mental state, emotion or feeling in the soul of the person. Because the average person has such a complex range of emotional states, there is an almost limitless range of auric shades and colors.[201]

THE THREE PRIMARY AURIC COLORS[202]

Like their physical counterparts, the auric colors are derived from three primary auric colors (red, blue and yellow), from which all the various combinations of colors are formed. These three primary colors, together with white and black, give us the key to the entire auric spectrum. Thus, the secondary colors are formed as follows:

- Green – derived from a combination of yellow and blue.
- Orange – from a combination of yellow and red.
- Purple – from a combination of red and blue.

Further combinations produce other colors. For example, green and purple form olive, orange and purple produce russet, and green and orange make citrine.

Black is really an absence of color, while white is essentially a harmonious blending of all colors. The blending of the primary colors in varied proportions produces hues of color. Similarly, adding white gives us tints, while mixing in black produces shades.

KEY TO AURIC COLORS[203]

An understanding of the basic character of the three primary auric colors, and of auric black and auric white, gives us the key to the whole range of auric coloring;

- The red group – represents the physical nature. As such, its presence indicates the existence and activity of that part of a person's nature.
- The blue group – represents the religious or spiritual nature.
- The yellow group – represents the intellectual nature.
- White – represents pure spirit.
- Black – represents the negation of pure spirit.

The various combinations of the three primary auric colors are formed when they are blended with each other or with white and black. These combinations result from the shades of mental and emotional activity that an individual manifests.

TABLE OF AURIC COLORS[204]

- Black – indicates hatred, malice, revenge, and similar low feelings.

- Gray:
    o Bright shades indicate selfishness.
    o Ghastly shades indicate fear and terror.
    o Dark shades indicate melancholy.

- Green:
    o Bright shades indicate diplomacy, worldly wisdom, suavity, tact, politeness, and polite deceit.
    o Dirty, muddy shades indicate low deceit, low cunning falsehood and trickery of a low order.
    o Dark, dull shades indicate jealousy, envy, and covetousness.

- Red is the color of passion, but there is a great variety in its manifestations. For example:
    o Dull red, appearing as if mixed with smoke, indicates sensuality and the lower animal passions.
    o Red appearing as bright flashes, sometimes lightning-like in form, indicates anger. The red often appears on a black background when the anger arises from hatred or malice, and on a greenish background when the anger arises from jealousy or envy. There tends to be no background color when the anger is the product of righteous indignation and the defense of what is believed to be a righteous cause.
    o Crimson represents love, and varies in shade according to the character of the passion. For instance, a dull, heavy shade indicates a gross and sensual love, while the brighter, clearer and more pleasing shades indicate love blended with higher feelings and accompanied by higher ideals.
    o Rose indicates the highest form of human love between the sexes.

- Brown (reddish shade) – indicates avarice and greed.

- Orange (bright shade) – represents pride and ambition.

- Yellow, in its various shades, represents intellectual power in its various forms:
    o A beautiful, clear, golden yellow indicates high intellectual attainment, logical reasoning, unprejudiced judgment and discernment.
    o A dark, dull yellow indicates intellectual power contenting itself with thoughts and subjects of a low, selfish order.
    o The shade between the two indicated above denotes the presence of higher or lower thought, respectively – the dark representing the lower, and the light, the higher.

- Blue:
    o Darker shades represent religious emotion, feeling and tendencies.
    o Dull shades indicate religious emotion of a low order, while the clearer brighter shades indicate religious emotions of a high order. The shades vary, ranging from indigo to a beautiful, bright violet.
    o Light, luminous, clear blue indicates spirituality. Within the auras of highly spiritual people, tiny luminous spark-like points are often visible, twinkling and sparkling like stars on a clear night.

AURIC COLORS IN PRACTICE[205]

If we focus our minds on a color, this will produce the feeling or emotion corresponding to that particular color. Thinking about one of the red group of colors, for example, may evoke in us strong, passionate feelings – as well as primal, animalistic emotions such as vitality, vigor and virility. Similarly, if we bring to mind the blue group, we will experience an uplift of spiritual or religious, emotional feelings. Again, if we wish to stimulate our intellectual faculties, or reinvigorate a tired mind, we need only concentrate on the yellow group of colors to obtain the desired result.

In other words, mental and emotional states manifest their corresponding colors, while colors tend to evoke their related mental and emotional states.

Having absorbed the idea of the aura, we must also understand the concept of the chakra.

CHAKRAS

Chakras are wheel-like vortices of different-colored energy. They are located where the three main energy channels in the human energy field cross. Think of them as the power station of the body: centers of activity that receive, assimilate, and express life force energy.[206]

There are three types of chakras. The lower, or animal, chakras are located between the toes and the pelvic region and relate to our evolutionary origins as part of the animal kingdom. The human chakras lie along the spinal column. Finally, the higher, or divine chakras, are found between the top of the spine and the crown of the head.[207]

The study of the chakras is central to many different therapies and disciplines, including aromatherapy, mantras, reiki, hands-on healing, flower essences, radionics, sound therapy, color/light therapy, and crystal/gem therapy. Other practices, including accupuncture, shiatsu, tai chi and chi kung, focus on balancing the energetic meridians that are an integral part of the chakra system, according to Vajrayana and Tantric Shakta theories.[208]

THE SEVEN MAJOR CHAKRAS[209]

Let's refer to figure 5 for a visual representation of the chakras.

1. Muladhara – The Base Chakra

Related to instinct, security, survival and basic human potentiality, the base chakra is located in the region between the genitals and the anus. Although no endocrine organ is located here, it is said to relate to the gonads and the adrenal medulla – responsible for the fight-or-flight survival instinct that is triggered when we are under threat.

There is a muscle located in this region that controls ejaculation in the human male. Muladhara is symbolized by a lotus with four petals and the color red. Key issues associated with this chakra are sexuality, lust and obsession. Physically, Muladhara governs sexuality, mentally it controls stability, emotionally it governs sensuality, and spiritually it is responsible for a sense of security.

2. Svadisthana – The Sacral Chakra

Located in the sacrum (hence the name), the Sacred Chakra corresponds to the testes or the ovaries that produce the various sex hormones involved in the reproductive cycle. Svadisthana is also considered to be related to, more generally, the genitourinary system and the adrenals. The Sacral Chakra is symbolized by a lotus with six petals, and corresponds to the color orange. The key issues involving Svadisthana are relationships, violence, addictions, basic emotional needs, and pleasure. Physically, Svadisthana governs reproduction, mentally it governs creativity, emotionally it governs joy, and spiritually it governs enthusiasm.

3. Manipura – The Solar Plexus Chakra

Related to the metabolic and digestive systems, Manipura corresponds to Islets of Langerhans – groups of cells in the pancreas – as well as the outer adrenal glands and the adrenal cortex. These play a valuable role in digestion and the conversion of food into energy for the body. Manipura is symbolized by a lotus with ten petals, and its associated color is yellow. Key issues governed by Manipura are personal power, fear, anxiety, opinion-formation, introversion, and the transition from simple or base emotions to complex. Physically, Manipura governs digestion, mentally it is responsible for personal power, emotionally it governs expansiveness, and spiritually, all matters of growth.

4. Anahata – The Heart Chakra

Anahata is related to the thymus, located in the chest. The thymus is an important element of the immune system, helping to create cells that ward of disease. It is, however, adversely affected by stress. Anahata is symbolized by a lotus flower with 12 petals and is related to green or pink. Anahata is involved with complex emotions, compassion, tenderness, unconditional love, equilibrium, rejection and wellbeing. Physically, Anahata governs circulation, emotionally it governs unconditional love for the self and others, mentally it governs passion, and spiritually it governs devotion.

5. Vishuddha – The Throat Chakra

Vishuddha relates to communication and growth through expression. This chakra is associated with the thyroid, a gland that is also in the throat and which produces the thyroid hormone, responsible for growth and maturation. Vishuddha is symbolized by a lotus with 16 petals, and characterized by light blue or turquoise. It governs such issues as self-expression and communication. Physically, Vishuddha governs communication, emotionally it governs independence, mentally it controls fluent thought, and spiritually, it helps to modulate our sense of security.

6. Ajna – The Brow Chakra

Ajna is linked to the pineal gland – a light-sensitive gland that produces the hormone melatonin, which regulates sleep and waking up. It is symbolized by a lotus with two petals, and corresponds to the colors white, indigo or deep blue. Ajna's key issues involve balancing the higher and lower selves and trusting inner guidance. Ajna's inner aspect relates to the access of intuition. Mentally, Ajna deals with visual consciousness, and emotionally, it deals with clarity on an intuitive level.

7. Sahasrara – The Crown Chakra

Widely considered to be the chakra of pure consciousness, Sahasrara relates to the pituitary gland, which communicates with the central nervous system through the thalamus – thought to have a key role in the physical basis of consciousness. Represented by a lotus with 1,000 petals, and the color violet, it is located at the crown of the head. Sahasrara involves such issues as inner wisdom and the death of the body. Its inner aspect deals with the release of karma, physical action with meditation, mental action with universal consciousness and unity, and emotional action with "beingness".

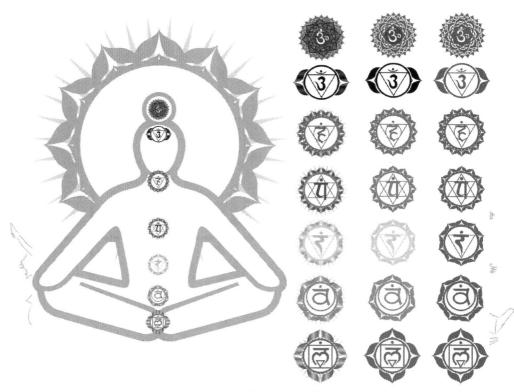

Figure 5. The chakras[210]

Unreleased emotions can lead to chakras becoming unbalanced and blocked, which can ultimately result in physical illness or disease. Below is a simple exercise to help prevent this from happening.

EXERCISE 20: CHAKRA BALANCING IN THREE PARTS[211]

Part 1 – Breathing exercise

- *Relax – slowly and deeply breathe in, then slowly breathe out. Relax every cell in your body starting with your scalp and face.*

- Slowly breathe in and tense the muscles in your scalp and face, then slowly breathe out and relax, feeling the tension drain away as you do so.

- Slowly breathe in and tense your neck muscles, then slowly breathe out and relax, feeling the tension drain away as you do so.

- Slowly breathe in and tense your shoulders, then slowly breathe out and relax, feeling the tension drain away as you do so.

- Slowly breathe in and tense your arms and hands, then slowly breathe out and relax, feeling the tension drain away as you do so.

- Slowly breathe in and tense your back and chest, then slowly breathe out and relax, feeling the tension drain away as you do so.

- Slowly breathe in and tense your buttocks, then slowly breathe out and relax, feeling the tension drain away as you do so.

- Slowly breathe in and tense your thighs and calf muscles, then slowly breathe out and relax, feeling the tension drain away as you do so.

- Slowly breathe in and tense your feet and ankles, then slowly breathe out and relax, feeling the tension drain away as you do so.

- Slowly breathe in, then slowly breathe out and relax any other tension, feeling it drain away as you breathe out.

- Bring your attention to your feet once again and visualize golden roots coming out of them, going deep down into Mother Earth, keeping you grounded and protected during the visualization. Now that you are completely relaxed, you are ready to begin.

Part 2 – Chakra color visualization

- Move your attention to the lower tip of your spine. This is where your base chakra is to be found. Visualize a wonderful RED flower slowly opening, bathing you in glorious vibrant RED. Soak up this brilliant RED energy until you feel you've had enough.

121

- Move your attention to the area halfway between your pubic bone and your belly button. This is where your sacral chakra is to be found. Visualize a wonderful ORANGE flower slowly opening, bathing you in glorious vibrant ORANGE. Soak up this brilliant ORANGE energy until you feel you've had enough.

- Move your attention to your solar plexus (stomach area just below the ribcage). This is where your solar plexus chakra is to be found. Visualize a wonderful YELLOW flower slowly opening, bathing you in glorious vibrant YELLOW. Soak up this brilliant YELLOW energy until you feel you've had enough.

- Move your attention to your heart area. This is where your heart chakra is to be found. Visualize a wonderful GREEN flower slowly opening, bathing you in glorious vibrant GREEN. Soak up this brilliant GREEN energy until you feel you've had enough.

- Move your attention to the middle of your throat. This is where your throat chakra is to be found. Visualize a wonderful BLUE flower slowly opening, bathing you in glorious vibrant BLUE. Soak up this brilliant BLUE energy until you feel you've had enough.

- Move your attention to the spot between your eyes. This is where your third eye chakra is to be found. Visualize a wonderful INDIGO flower slowly opening, bathing you in glorious vibrant INDIGO. Soak up this brilliant INDIGO energy until you feel you've had enough.

- Move you attention to the top of your head. This is where your crown chakra is to be found. Visualize a wonderful VIOLET flower slowly opening, bathing you in glorious vibrant VIOLET. Soak up this brilliant VIOLET energy until you feel you've had enough.

- Bathe in the RAINBOW beauty of your open chakras for a couple of minutes.

Part 3 – Chakra closure

- Bring your attention to your RED base chakra flower. Visualize all the petals closing and withdrawing back into your body.

- Next move up to your ORANGE sacral chakra flower. Visualize all the petals closing and withdrawing back into your body.

- Next move up to your YELLOW solar plexus chakra flower. Visualize all the petals closing and withdrawing back into your body.

- Next move up to your GREEN heart chakra flower. Visualize all the petals closing and withdrawing back into your body.

- Next move up to your BLUE throat chakra flower. Visualize all the petals closing and withdrawing back into your body.

- Next move up to your INDIGO third eye chakra. Visualize all the petals closing and withdrawing back into your body.

- Next move up to your VIOLET crown chakra. Visualize all the petals closing and withdrawing back into your body.

- To finish the session and bring it to a close, visualize yourself standing under a waterfall of white light for a couple of minutes. Then, when you feel ready, come back in your body and fully into the present by wriggling your fingers and toes. Then open your eyes, and gently stretch.

This exercise will help you feel the different energies in your chakras. With practice, you will begin to sense how long to spend at each center.

Make a conscious effort to be aware of your energetic system. Whatever you observe in your physical body derives from the state of your energetic body.

June – Mental Healing

Every human being is the author of his or her own health or disease.[212]

BUDDHA

MENTAL HEALING

Mental healing means mind healing. The ability to heal physical illness and disease through the power of right thinking is based on the theory that we are surrounded by an infinite mind that reacts to our thoughts. It is only when we understand that everything is mind, and that the only instrument of mind is contemplative thought that we can fully appreciate why right thinking alone has the power to permanently heal.[213]

Thoughts become our physical reality, therefore thoughts of sickness will make a person sick. Conversely, thoughts of health and perfection will heal them. This is because when thought is combined with belief and conviction it becomes a powerful tool with which to treat ourselves and others.[214]

DISEASE IS A MENTAL CONSTRUCT

Sickness, disease and injury are all fundamentally a product of the mind, not our physical bodies. When the life principle leaves the body, it becomes what we call a corpse – a lifeless and inanimate form. It can no longer become sick because there is no mental activity there to generate the reality of illness.[215]

Illness cannot manifest unless an intelligence is present that is capable of recognizing and feeling it. Disease is primarily a mental construct.

In other words, without mentality, it is not and yet with mentality, it appears to be.[216]

For instance, a disease may be contagious between two living people; but it cannot pass between two dead people. There must be intelligence present, even within a contagious disease, for the body to contract it. Similarly, the dead body cannot catch the disease from the living because the intelligence has departed.[217]

DISEASE IS NOT ALWAYS THE RESULT OF CONSCIOUS THOUGHT

Disease is not necessarily the product of conscious thought; it can also be created by our subconscious mind; or it may be the result of many thoughts which, when combined, produce a tangible result.[218]

Disease cannot appear in the body unless it has first appeared as an image in the mind. In fact, the vast majority of physical illnesses originate not from conscious thought but in our subconscious thoughts, which subsequently reveal themselves externally as symptoms. A related group of thoughts will combine to produce a particular illness, which, in most instances, will not have been anticipated by the sufferer.[219]

HOW TO TREAT A PATIENT

Knowing that illness derives from subconscious thought means that when we practice healing we must treat physical conditions as illnesses of the mind.[220]

Diseases can be cured provided we can isolate and remove the root cause (which will be a mental condition). Of course, this assumes that the patient is amenable to treatment. You cannot heal someone if you suspect their condition stems from a mental attitude they are unwilling to abandon. But as a practitioner, it is your duty to uncover false ideas and replace them with the truth. Accordingly, you must seek to identify these negative thoughts and encourage the patient to confront why it is they are clinging to them. If this can be done before the disease destroys the body, healing will always follow.[221]

When healing someone, you shouldn't simply hope, ask, or desire that your patient gets well, you must also actively generate an understanding at the forefront of your conscious mind that the patient is healed and is perfect.[222]

If your thoughts are clear and you are able to consciously realize the presence of Spirit in your patient, your healing powers will know no bounds.[223]

To practice metaphysical healing, you must first become aware that you are dealing with a universal principle, or law, whereby your thoughts have consequences in the physical realm. Once you have accepted this, nothing can stop you.[224]

REMOTE HEALING USING YOUR MIND

As an individual, your mind is part of one universal subjective mind, without which metaphysical treatment would be impossible. Without one unifying mind, there would be no common medium through which to work, think or act. Since there is only one subjective mind and we are always thinking into it, then whether a patient is present or absent makes no difference.[225]

Metaphysical healing does not treat bodies or conditions, because we are dealing only with thought. Consequently, there is no need for physical contact with a patient, nor does the patient need to be hypnotized before treatment can take effect. In fact, where the patient is and what they are doing is irrelevant. As a healer, your work begins and ends within your own consciousness.[226]

REALIZING PERFECTION

Healing is accomplished not through willpower alone but by knowing the truth; this truth is that we are already perfect (see January – Self-Love) – no matter what appearances may suggest.[227]

A person suffering from an illness will remain sick until the healer knows that the patient is well. Because the mind of the healer and that of the patient are all part of the same universal mind, they occupy and operate within the same medium, which means the healer's thoughts can reach out to the sick person and help him or her.

Your role as a healer is to realize the salient truth for your patient within yourself. When this happens, this knowledge can then begin to permeate the consciousness of the patient. Think of it as planting a seed in the ground: as a practitioner, you sow the seed and the creative mind produces the plant.[228]

However, as a healer, before you can transfer this awareness to the patient via the universal mind, you must first treat yourself. You cannot erase the relevant negative thought in the patient's mentality until you have first neutralized that thought in your own mind. What you are doing, in effect, is to take your patient, their disease and everything else that appears to be wrong and absorb it into your own mentality. It is only by doing this that you can dissolve all false appearances and wrong conclusions. In other words, you deal with the condition not as reality but as a belief. This in turn eradicates the false thought at the very core of your being, thus healing the condition. The more completely you believe in your own thoughts, the more power your healing will have. The person whose consciousness is the clearest and who has the most complete idea of life will be the best healer.[229]

Treatment must be specific. If you are treating someone against their belief in scarlet fever, for example, your thoughts must serve to neutralize a belief in this disease. During treatment you must conceive of everything – bodies, objects, people, etc. – as thoughts. Having done so, you must then understand that disease is neither person, place nor thing; it has no location, belongs to no one, cannot operate through anyone, is not believed by anyone. You must realize that the disease is a false belief, a false image, with no power. Know that the whole thing is a mental construct; then mentally dissolve it.[230]

In treating someone who appears to be insane, understand that there is but one mind and it is perfect; it contains your mind and that of your patient. They are one and the same. This mind, being complete, perfect and indivisible, is free of delusion and falseness. After you have understood this, realize that this is also true about your patient; their thought is also perfect. If you hold this to be fundamentally true, there can be no doubts or confusion and the mind of the patient will cease to be deranged.[231]

Healing is not about creating the perfect body or the perfect idea, it is about revealing an idea which is already perfect. Healing is not a process, it is a revelation through the thought of the healer to the thought of the patient. There is a process involved *within* healing, but there is not a process *of* healing. The process involved in healing is the mental work you initially have to do as a healer to convince yourself of the perfection of your patient. And finally, it is the work the patient has to do to realize this perfection.[232]

NEVER TREAT THE BODY

Never think of a sick person as someone who simply has a sick body, because the cause of the disease is not in the body. The body is an effect, not a cause. Bodies and the conditions that affect them are passive; they are always acted upon. A sick person is someone who has a sick thought.[233]

Nor should you treat the disease as belonging to the person. If you do, the disease becomes an integral part of them. As a healer, you must think of the patient as a person born of spirit, not of matter. And because spirit is changeless, perfect, complete, and in every respect pure, inviolate and uncontaminated, the person you are seeking to heal is by definition a living embodiment of perfection.[234]

Your thoughts can literally heal another person, providing the right kind of thinking is consistently applied. In the periods between treatments, do not carry the thought of the patient around with you. To do so is to allow doubts to creep in which may undo all the good work you have done. Each treatment should instead be an affirmation of the reality of being and should be repeated daily until the patient is no longer sick.[235]

Using the information provided above we can construct a practical exercise for healing.

EXERCISE 21: MENTAL HEALING

1. *Contemplation: Bring yourself to the meditative state using whatever method works best for you (see October – Awareness). Be convinced of your own perfection. You can use the affirmation "I am – divine perfection" meditation on an inhale-exhale basis.*

2. *Visualization: Form a picture in your mind of the current state of your patient's body, including their erroneous notion of the physical condition or pain that is bothering them. Use simplified pictures to help your mind grasp more readily what it is you are dealing with. For example, if you are treating a kidney complaint you could visualize the kidneys as a pair of butter beans. Remember, this is not the "real" state, merely a state that has been formed due to wrong thinking that you are working to neutralize.*

3. *Neutralization: Visualize the physical problem disappearing. Create in your mind a system to remove the condition. For example, if you are treating kidney stones you may want to visualize them being crushed into powder that is then safely removed. Whatever image you create in your mind will be correct as long as it is speaking to your subconscious mind. This must be a process you feel familiar with and in whose positive results you wholeheartedly believe in.*

4. *Realizing perfection for your patient: Let the final picture of your visualization be one of perfect health. Feel the joy of perfect health for the person you are treating. Use affirmations (see October – Awareness) to reinforce what you do. Believe the healing process to be powerful and already occurring. Never doubt the effectiveness of your mental work. Expect the reality to be created exactly how you have visualized it.*

5. *Coming out of meditation: Detach from what you have been doing and come out of your meditative state. Know that the healing action is taking place. Realize that you have performed a magical act.*

AURIC HEALING

The aura (see May – Energy, Auras and Chakras) is the electrical magnetic energy that emanates from the human body. Auric healing involves changing a person's condition by *visualizing* a specific colored light around them. The colors are chosen according to the person's condition.

Different colors heal different afflictions:

THERAPEUTIC SCALE OF COLORS[236]

Colors may be applied in therapeutic work either by being physically placed in the environment of the person you are treating or by you visualizing them:

- Blues, violet, and lavender have a cooling, soothing effect on the nervous system and on the blood and bodily organs.
- Grass greens have a restful, invigorating effect on the same.
- Yellows and orange have an inspiring, illuminating effect on the mind.
- Reds have an exciting, stimulating effect on mind and body (this is particularly true of scarlets and other bright reds).[237]

Let's examine some specific examples:

- If a patient is complaining of flu, or claims to be suffering from stress, visualize that person completely surrounded by, and absorbed in, **blue** light.

- For someone with a nervous headache or a disease of the eyes or ears, picture that person's head surrounded by **violet or lavender** light.

- If a patient has a stomach pain or an ulcer, then direct a soothing **green** color to the affected areas.

- For someone suffering from depression or fatigue, envision them surrounded by **orange.**

- **Red** should be used for treating anemia or a cold.

131

I am obliged to state that the mental healing methods I have outlined above should never be used as a replacement for a visit to the doctor.

THE MYSTERIOUS PLACEBO EFFECT

Scientists and doctors have long been puzzled by how patients have sometimes been able to heal themselves of life-threatening diseases. In some instances, patients have triggered the self-healing process simply by believing they will be cured. This is commonly known as the placebo effect.[238]

In medical studies, people have been cured of illness after taking fake medication (placebos) – usually nothing more than sugar pills or colored, distilled water – that their doctor has told them beforehand is real medication.[239]

There is no wholly satisfactory explanation for why the placebo effect works, but it is widely accepted that somehow the patient's belief that they are being cured activates an inherent self-healing ability.

The placebo effect is one of the best-documented ways in which the mind is known to affect the body.[240] Its potential power is so great that all new drugs now have to be tested against a placebo before they can be approved for public use. Indeed, many former treatments and drugs have been taken off the market when their healing properties were found to be solely due to the placebo effect.

All this leads to an interesting question: to what extent is our physical body influenced by the belief systems our minds create? The answer, suggested by the evidence presented in this chapter, is that the gap between mind and body is non-existent.

CONCLUSION

Because we are all interconnected, the way in which a person thinks about someone else affects not only the person who is thinking those thoughts but everybody else. Most people are unaware that the universe is a mental construct and that what we think influences everyone and everything around us. Therefore, their thoughts tend to be scattered and diluted.

Knowing the power of your own thoughts can have an immense impact on yourself and others – for good or for evil. On a global scale, if all humanity suddenly started having only wholesome, positive, healthy and loving thoughts, there would be no disease, there would be no crime, no war, no harm whatsoever. While we cannot change the thoughts of all humanity immediately, we can nevertheless make a start by doing so ourselves, knowing that we are all connected. By changing our thoughts into wholesome, loving ones, we can truly make the world a better place.

July – Subliminal Messages

Whatever we plant in our subconscious mind and nourish with repetition and emotion will one day become a reality.[241]

EARL NIGHTINGALE

Sigmund Freud said: "The conscious mind may be compared to a fountain playing in the sun and falling back into the great subterranean pool of subconscious from which it rises."[242] The subconscious mind is a field of consciousness. Every thought impulse that reaches the objective mind through any of the five senses is classified and recorded here, and may be recalled or withdrawn in the same way that documents may be taken from a filing cabinet. It receives, and files, sense impressions or thoughts, regardless of their nature. Thoughts that you have consciously planted in your subconscious mind are transformed into physical reality. These can involve money, people, a job – whatever your heart desires. The subconscious acts first on thoughts with the strongest resonance: those that have been imbued with powerful emotion, such as faith.[243]

The subconscious mind works continuously, throughout the day and night, using the power of infinite intelligence to translate your desires into physical reality.[244]

Affecting lasting change in yourself requires you to access the subliminal (subconscious) part of your mind.[245] Subliminal programming is an excellent way to do this. Through the use of subliminal messages you can bypass the conscious mind and reprogram your inner mind.

SUBLIMINAL MESSAGES AND ADVERTISING[246]

Subliminal messages are affirmations that are given just below the threshold of conscious awareness. They are used to program the subconscious mind or influence subconscious behavior. This means that anything that is deliberately given to you at a subconscious level in order to change your perspective, outlook, behavior or beliefs is a subliminal message.

Many people believe that subliminal messages are images that are invisible to you, or voices that cannot be heard. This is far from the truth. They are merely hidden or masked behind other things, as in figure 6. To be effective, they must be visible and they must be audible. For example, subliminal messages in advertising usually involve masking images or words so that they blend in with their background and only become apparent when they are pointed out, looked for, or accidentally noticed. The subliminal messages must be visible or else they would not work. The same applies to subliminal messages in recordings. The auditory subliminal messages must be clear and easy to hear if the other sounds are removed. This is the reason so many subliminal messages in audios are hidden behind music. They mask or hide the subliminal messages so that you cannot consciously make out what is being said, or even determine if it is actually a voice. Take away the music, however, and you would clearly hear the subliminal messages.

The effectiveness of subliminal messages is due to the way your mind works. You can only consciously concentrate on a finite number of things at any one time. However, your subconscious mind is aware of millions of things happening all at once. This is vital for two reasons. First, your ability to block out almost all of the stimuli that are reaching your senses allows you to remain focused on what you are doing. If everything that is happening around you were to become apparent to you at once, you would have sensory overload and be unable to function efficiently at any given task. The only time other stimuli come into your conscious awareness is when they require your attention. It is then that the subconscious mind alerts the conscious mind of this stimulus. Second, you have learned to walk, talk and drive consciously. Yet, when you perform these tasks now, you access your subconscious programs and run them automatically. This frees up your conscious mind to do other things. Once you consciously learn something, it is passed into the subconscious mind for storage and retrieval. The same applies to your current predominate thoughts, attitudes and feelings.

Most of your beliefs and attitudes have been formed over many years and will have been critically analyzed and tested throughout your life. These beliefs and attitudes are stored in your subconscious mind and accessed as you need them. The subconscious mind is an obedient servant to the conscious mind. In fact, it is merely a storehouse of information, feelings and beliefs. It cannot analyze or decide what it does or does not hold. It accepts as fact everything that it receives. To program the subconscious with stored information, it is usually necessary for the information to pass through the conscious mind, where it can be analyzed, then accepted or rejected.

The conscious mind therefore acts as gatekeeper to the subconscious mind. However, the subconscious mind can be influenced without interference from the conscious mind through the use of subliminal messages. This can be used to influence behavior, beliefs and attitudes, so needs to be something that you alone are in control of.

Advertisers have known about the power of subliminal messages for decades and use them to fire your emotions and sway your buying habits. By embedding subliminal messages into ads, they can help plant in your subconscious mind a connection between their product and a pleasurable feeling, belief or physical drive. In a similar way, you can use the power of subliminal messages to reprogram your mind with new beliefs, attitudes, skills and feelings.

———

There is mounting evidence to suggest that subliminal messages affect us at a deep level. A book written in 1958 by Wilson Bryan Key, *Subliminal Seduction,* claims that subliminal techniques had been widely used in advertising. If you take a look at YouTube, you can see many examples of subliminal messages being widely used in advertising today.

Figure 6. Subliminal messages[247]

Subliminal messages can be of various types:

TEXTUAL SUBLIMINAL MESSAGES

The possibilities, and acceptable boundaries, of subliminal advertising have long been the subject of debate. In 1957, market researcher James Vicary claimed to have increased sales of popcorn by almost 60 per cent, and of Coca-Cola by almost 20 per cent through subliminal presentation of the slogans "Drink Coca-Cola" and "Eat Popcorn" in the movie *Picnic* in Fort Lee, New Jersey.[248] By 1962, this claim had been exposed as a publicity hoax, but the story lives on in advertising industry infamy.[249]

Vicary's study has never been replicated, however other experiments since then seem to suggest Vicary's fantasies have some basis in reality. In 2006 Johan Karremans, PhD and colleagues from the Department of Social Psychology in Radboud University Nijmegen in the Netherlands, published two experiments, which assessed whether subliminal priming of a brand name of a drink can affect people's choices for the primed brand, and whether this effect is moderated by individuals' feelings of thirst. Both studies demonstrated that subliminal priming of a brand name of a drink (Lipton Ice and Spa Rood – a Dutch brand of mineral water) positively affected participants' preference for, and intention to drink, the primed brand, but only among participants who were thirsty.[250]

The results obtained by Karremans and his team were confirmed by a joint group of scientists from Saarland University, Germany, and the School of Psychology, University of Western Australia. For their study, published in 2009, they adapted Karremans' et al's paradigm to the concept of "concentration" and embedded the subliminal presentation of a brand logo into a computer game. Subsequent consumption of sugar pills (of a presented or not presented brand) was measured dependent on the level of participants' tiredness and the subliminally presented logo. The scientists found the same pattern as Karremans et al: only tired participants consumed more of the subliminally presented than the not presented brand. This research therefore suggests that we are influenced by subliminally presented stimuli if these stimuli are need-related and if we are in a corresponding motivational state.[251]

To be processed, subliminal verbal primes have to consist of one or perhaps two (very short) words, but not whole sentences.[252] This was evident in a pictorial advertisement that portrays four different types of rum. The phrase "U Buy" was embedded backwards in the picture. A study was done to test the effectiveness of the alcohol ad. Before the study, participants were told to try to identify a hidden message in the ad. None found any. Eventually, 80 per cent of the subjects unconsciously perceived the backward message, meaning they showed a preference for that particular brand of rum.[253]

As only a single word or image can be effectively perceived, the simpler the features of that image or word (i.e. food relates to hunger) the more effective the resulting change in behavior will be. This was demonstrated in a study where the word "beef" was flashed for several, five millisecond intervals during a 16-minute movie shown to experimental subjects, while nothing was flashed to controlled subjects. Afterwards, neither the experimental nor controlled subjects reported a higher preference for beef sandwiches when shown a list of five different foods, but the experimental subjects did rate themselves as hungrier than the controlled subjects when questioned. However, if the subjects were flashed a whole sentence, the words would not be perceived and no effect would be expected.[254]

Textual subliminal messages have been allegedly used on many occasions, including during the 2000 US Presidential election campaign, when a 30-second television advertisement campaign for Republican candidate George W. Bush focused on one of the main domestic issues of the campaign: the provision of prescription drugs for the elderly. The ad, which had been broadcast in several key states, said senior citizens would have more control over their healthcare under Mr Bush's proposals than Vice-President Al Gore's. "The Gore prescription plan – bureaucrats decide. The Bush prescription plan – seniors choose," the ad says.[255] It also included an image of Gore, followed by fragments of the words "Bureaucrats decide". The word "rats" briefly flashes on the screen before the entire word "bureaucrats" appears.[256]

Gore's aides seized on the ad as evidence of a dirty tricks campaign. Bush, however, denied that his team planted the word "rats" as a subliminal message in the ad in order to smear his Democrat opponent.[257]

IMAGE SUBLIMINAL MESSAGES

In 1992, two studies involving 162 undergraduates demonstrated that attitudes can develop without an awareness of their antecedents. Individuals viewed slides of people performing familiar daily activities after being exposed to either an emotionally positive scene such as a romantic couple or kittens, or an emotionally negative scene such as a werewolf or a dead body between each slide. After exposure, which the individuals consciously perceived as a flash of light, participants attributed more positive personality traits to those people whose slides were associated with an emotionally positive scene, and vice-versa.[258]

A team from University College, London, used brain scans to confirm that people do register subliminal images, but only if the brain had "spare capacity". The researchers cited the example of the movie *Fight Club*, where a character who works as a cinema projectionist inserts a single frame of pornography into the 24 frames of a film shown each second. In the movie, those watching were unaware of the split-second shot, but felt depressed or aggressive afterwards.[259]

Their study included seven participants who wore red-blue filter glasses that projected faint images of everyday objects onto one eye and an emotive, flashing image onto the other. The flashing image meant the participants were not consciously aware of the faint images projected onto the other eye. At the same time, they were asked to carry out an easy task, such as picking out the letter "T" from a stream of letters, or a harder task of picking out a white "N" or a blue "Z".[260]

Using brain scanning, the researchers found that during the easy task the brain registered the "invisible" object, although participants were unaware they had seen it. This was highlighted by activity in a part of the brain called the primary visual cortex. But during the harder task, which required more concentration, the brain scan did not pick up any relevant brain activity, suggesting the participants had not registered the subliminal image.[261]

Dr Bahador Bahrami, of the UCL Institute of Cognitive Neuroscience, said: "What's interesting here is that your brain does log things that you are not even aware of and cannot ever become aware of. The brain is open to what's around it. So if there is spare capacity, in terms of attention, the brain will allocate that resource to subliminal activity. These findings point to the sort of impact that subliminal advertising may have on the brain."[262]

Numerous companies use subliminal messages to influence our perception of their brands, our feelings attached to them and, ultimately, our choice. Let's have a look at some examples.

One of the many instances of fast food multinational McDonald's use of subliminal messages was during the television cooking show *Iron Chef*. It was just one quick flash of the McDonald's logo across the screen, which was almost imperceptible to the naked eye. Indeed, most viewers would have thought it was merely the result of faulty reception that the screen flashed yellow and red. The conscious mind wouldn't have even been able to pick up the logo. However, the subconscious mind has no problem picking it up. The end result of this is to cause viewers to associate McDonald's with good food like that featured on *Iron Chef*. [263]

Another example of subliminal communication was an ad for the fast food giant KFC that superimposed a dollar bill on a KFC-brand sandwich. It is something that you would never consciously have noticed unless you zoomed in on it. However, the subconscious mind spots this straight away. KFC's rationale would be that you will subsequently associate value and good feelings with their sandwich just like you do with your money.

Disney is also famous for inserting subliminal messages in its movies, some of which it has acknowledged and some of which it hasn't. One example that Disney admitted to is the photographic image that can be spotted in the background of the 1977 animated movie *The Rescuers*. In January 1999, Disney recalled 3.4 million home video copies of this movie, saying two frames contain an "objectionable background image". [264]

According to sources quoted by the Associated Press, the film contains a photo of a naked woman. In a statement, a spokeswoman for Disney said the images (two frames) in *The Rescuers* were placed in the film during production, although she declined to say what they were or who placed them there, and claimed they cannot be seen in ordinary viewing because the film runs too fast. [265]

The Rescuers is the first video ever to be recalled by the company for having an objectionable image. The company said it had made the recall to protect its reputation as a trusted, family-friendly brand.[266]

Several other Disney movies allegedly contain questionable images and sounds, including *The Little Mermaid*, *Aladdin* and *The Lion King*.

The Exorcist was also at the center of controversy due to its alleged use of subliminal imagery. An article in the July/August 1991 issue of *Video Watchdog* investigated the claims, and featured still frames from the film that it claimed constituted subliminal "flashing". In an interview in the same issue, the movie's director, William Friedkin said: "I saw subliminal cuts in a number of films before I ever put them in *The Exorcist*, and I thought it was a very effective storytelling device... The subliminal editing in *The Exorcist* was done for dramatic effect – to create, achieve, and sustain a kind of dreamlike state." However, these split-second images have been labeled "[not] truly subliminal" and "quasi-" or "semi-subliminal" because true subliminal imagery must be, by definition, below the threshold of awareness. A 1999 book about *The Exorcist* featured an interview with William Blatty, the author of the novel on which the movie is based. When asked about the controversy, he insisted: "There are no subliminal images. If you can see it, it's not subliminal."[267]

———

Another interesting subliminal concept can be observed in several logos:

FedEx: FedEx Corporation is a multinational delivery company.[268] Its logo, one of the most recognized in the world, seems innocuous enough. However, if you look carefully you'll notice it features a right-pointing arrow located in the blank space between the "E" and the "X". Most people wouldn't notice it unless it were pointed out to them. The arrow subliminally conveys the message of forward movement, direction, speed and reliability.[269]

Virgin: Virgin Group has interests in a wide range of areas, chiefly travel, entertainment and lifestyle.[270] If you turn the Virgin logo slightly to the left, the underline and tail of the "g" form an "x". You'll also notice that the "V" forms a slightly hidden "s", and the "I", "r" and top part of the "g" form a broken capital "e", spelling the word "sex". So you have "sex" and "Virgin" in one word. Our subconscious mind can perceive the hidden word "sex" and we then attribute all the pleasures we associate with sex with the Virgin brand.

Amazon: Amazon is an online bookstore that ships its products, which now include many other products besides books, all over the world. Its famous logo is very clean and simple in design, but the arrow underneath the word "Amazon", which extends from the "A" to the "z", may be subtly suggesting that amazon.com has everything from a to z, while its curved shape may represent the smile brought to the customer's face. I hope you are smiling now, especially if you purchased this book at amazon.com!

The above are just a few examples, but there are many more – just look around. Research shows that our brains process subtle information without our conscious awareness, and this may also be the case with subliminal logos.

Manufactures go to great lengths to get around bans on the advertising of their products. In Formula One racing, for example, tobacco advertising has been prohibited in many of the competing countries. But the color schemes of many cars carry jokey messages intended to look like, or suggest, banned tobacco brands. For example, Jordan Grand Prix ran Benson & Hedges sponsorship as "Bitten & Hisses", with a snake-skin design on the body of their cars. A similar procedure was used by NASCAR driver Jeff Burton after AT&T Mobility advertising was banned by a court order in 2007, and by Penske Championship Racing in NASCAR (where Cellco Partnership is prohibited) and the IRL (Marlboro). In these instances, a distinctive design featuring the banned company's identity (the Verizon "V" and the Marlboro chevron) was integrated into the car's design.[271]

AUDIO SUBLIMINAL MESSAGES

Audio messages can be recorded either forward (so that if you were to make the main audible element silent, you would be able to hear the embedded message in the background) or backwards – backmasking. During the 1970s, media reports raised a series of concerns about its possible impact on listeners, stating that embedded satanic messages were urging listeners to commit suicide, murder, abuse drugs, or engage in sex – the rates of which were increasing at the time.[272]

There have probably been thousands of albums produced that contain subliminal lyrics. Some bands do this openly, as in *Masterhit,* by Front 242, which is included on the Backwards Masking website. Pitch Shifter, a band known for incorporating technology into their music, have been featuring backwards sounds in their songs for years. On their 1996 album *Infotainment?,* they even included two tracks of featured backmasked lyrics. The first track, "Introductory Disclaimer", begins with a voice explaining, essentially, that a subliminal message is about to be played. It then proceeds to play soft, sinuous string music in which the words "Pitch Shifter are good: Pitch Shifter are our pals" are embedded, quite noticeably. The second occurrence, "(Harmless) Interlude" on track six, contains the same lyrics and music. In contrast to this overt, light-hearted display of backmasking, the band Judas Priest was taken to court for allegedly using subliminal lyrics to urge listeners to commit suicide.

For many years, retailers have been playing subliminal tapes in stores to persuade shoppers to buy their products. Some websites offer tapes of upbeat jazz or Latino music, embedded within which are recorded messages designed to persuade consumers to spend, or deter them from stealing. "Don't worry about the money!" or "Imagine owning it!" accompany other audio messages such as "Buy now and don't take it, you'll get caught!" According to one vendor of such materials, sales increased by 15 per cent and thefts decreased by 58 per cent among stores who used the tapes.[273]

There is a vast array of companies offering self-help audio materials that claim to help you attract into your life the things you seek: build self-esteem and self-confidence, help you to relax, lose weight, improve your relationships, overcome fears and phobias, improve your physical wellbeing, enhance athleticism, sharpen up memory skills and enhance creative thoughts, boost IQ, overcome addictions such as smoking, and many, many others. You can even find alleged scientific proof of the effectiveness of subliminal recording on the websites of the companies offering this panacea of self-help, although this usually consists of little more than a few vaguely worded sentences. For example, they quote Vicary's story as the reason WHY you should use their products. As we have seen at the beginning of this chapter, Vicary's claim to have increased sales of Coca-Cola and popcorn was exposed as a hoax. Also, it referred to flashing messages on the screen and not to audio messages.

I am not saying that these subliminal recordings do not work – quite the opposite: I want to believe that they do work. However, having learned in one scientific paper that Vicary's study was a hoax and viewing one subliminal sales website where this hoax is the main marketing tool used to promote their subliminal audios, I continue to believe *only what I myself have tested and judged to be true.*

A double-blind test of subliminal self-help audiotapes was conducted by a team of scientists from several US universities. Three replications of a double-blind experiment tested subliminal audiotape products that claimed to improve memory or to increase self-esteem. Test conditions conformed to manufacturers' recommendations, and the 237 participants were all individuals who sought the effects offered by the tapes. Actual content and labeled content of tapes were independently varied, so that some subjects who believed they were using memory tapes were actually using self-esteem tapes, and vice-versa. After a month's use (the point at which users should notice results, according to the manufacturers), neither the memory nor the self-esteem tapes produced their claimed effects. Nevertheless, a general improvement for all subjects in both memory and self-esteem was observed, and more than a third of the subjects had the illusion of improvement in the area specified on the tape's label.[274]

The fact that the result of this particular experiment was negative does not prove that subliminal audio does not work; it only proves that subliminal audio of those particular tapes tested on those particular subjects did not work.

In order to have a valid experiment we would need to test several factors:

- The presence of the subliminal message. We must be sure that there is in fact a message recorded on the tapes, as there have been several claims of dishonest producers selling "subliminal" recordings with no message recorded whatsoever.

- Length of subliminal message. There have been claims that only messages composed of one or two short words have an effect; too long messages allegedly do not work.

- Loudness of subliminal message. The threshold at which we do not hear the message, yet our subconscious does, must be established at a plausible level.

- Genre of music. The music itself could impact the experiment, therefore we need to understand whether certain types of music could have a stronger effect than others.

- Reliability of participants. The experiment must be "lazy proof". In other words, we must be sure the participants of the experiment have listened to the recording in the frequency demanded by the manufacturer.

- The motivation of the participants. In the experiment described above, only motivated individuals were tested. However, in a further study, this element should also be taken into consideration.

To conclude, we may want to believe that subliminal audio is an effective self-help tool. And, as we have seen, belief alone is often enough for it to work. But to establish this link conclusively, more scientific research is needed – a process that promises to be exhilarating.

———

As mentioned before, pop music, movies, advertisements are packed with subliminal messages. If you still doubt their effectiveness, ask yourself why the advertising industry spends such incredible amounts of money to create them and insert them in their campaigns.

Just as many companies use subliminal advertising to persuade you to buy their products, in a similar way, assuming that subliminal messages are effective, you can use their power to reprogram your mind with new beliefs, attitudes, skills and feelings. By using subliminal messages you can begin to program yourself and change your attitudes and actions in a way that helps you. I'm sure you will agree that it is preferable to have subliminal messages reaching your inner mind that *you* have chosen, and which will therefore help you to create the beliefs, attitudes and actions that will create the life you want.

As demonstrated earlier, there are numerous claims that subliminal messages do not work. If we assume that there is no evidence that subliminal messages work, then why do several countries ban them from being used in advertising?

As in many other areas, it seems scientists do not agree with one another. But do they have to? After all, we still know so little about the power of the brain. Furthermore, we are all different and respond differently to different stimuli. One man's meat is another man's poison. The best way to find out what works for us is to try different things out.

Believe only what you yourself test and judge to be true. If a certain method doesn't work for you, you gain precious knowledge that it is a waste of time and you should allocate your energy elsewhere. If it does work, it means that you have just discovered an incredible way to create your reality and achieve whatever you desire. By bypassing the conscious mind and speaking directly with the subconscious, you truly are a master of mind.

To conclude, on the one hand, there is little research proving the effectiveness of subliminal messages. On the other hand, we know that subliminal stimuli are widely used in advertising, movies, politics, songs, etc. Without making any controversial statements, I would like to leave the interpretation of this phenomenon to the reader, together with the following exercise.

EXERCISE 22: MASTER YOUR THOUGHTS SUBLIMINALLY

Become the master of you own thoughts, influence your subconscious mind subliminally to become whatever you desire.

Further research the subject to develop your own point of view. Investigate textual, image, and audio messages.

Share your findings on the "Master of Thought" website at www.master-of-thought.com. Visit regularly to be updated on the latest mind-expanding techniques.

August – Infinite Possibility, Interconnection, Limitlessness

INFINITE POSSIBILITY

Matrix character: *Every program that is created must have a purpose. If it does not, it is deleted.*

Agent Smith (computer program): *Without purpose we would not exist. It is purpose that created us, purpose that connects us, purpose that pulls us, that guides us, that drives us. It is purpose that defines us, purpose that binds us.*

THE MATRIX

He might have added: *It is purpose that controls us.*[275]

Let us state the obvious – sometimes this is necessary because we overlook it:

*To be infinite possibility, we need to **be** infinite possibility. We cannot be infinite possibility by being anything less than that. To identify with a single possibility is not to encompass all into oneness.*[276]

So far, we have seen that through the law of vibration we can control our reality through right thinking. We can bring into existence everything we wish when we make a conscious effort to think correctly.[277]

Through right thinking and conscious creation, poverty, disease, unhappiness and all the other problems that blight our existence can be wiped off the face of the Earth. Of course, not everybody believes this but those who do and comply with the law of vibration have proven it to be true.[278]

Each and every one of us in the world today has the power to transform our own environment by striving to create our own reality.[279]

If we live according to the law of vibration, comply with its nature and consistently apply right thinking and living, our lives will be more complete and fulfilling than we could ever have imagined. The law always works in accordance with the belief of those seeking to use it. Just as the universe is run by an infinite mind, our lives are controlled by our thought. Ignorance enslaves us, yet knowledge can free us.[280]

EXERCISE 23: LIVING AS INFINITE POSSIBILITY

Live, talk, think and act believing that there is a limitless power accompanying you on your journey through life; directing and guiding your every action into expressions of peace, health, happiness and harmony.

You alone have the power to determine how you live your life, how successful you are, and how happy – provided that you first obey the Law and learn how to make conscious use of it.[281]

INTERCONNECTION

We are united with the Whole. A drop of water is not the ocean, yet it contains within itself all the attributes of the limitless deep.[282]

Our subconscious mind merges with the universal subjective mind and influences our thoughts to produce the sparks of creativity.[283]

This creative power has been the greatest discovery in human history. This same force can make us sick and yet can heal us. Equally well, it has the power to make us miserable or happy.[284]

To become prosperous, we must first become conscious of prosperity; if we want to be healthy, we must embody the idea of health. A consciousness of health, happiness and prosperity can be induced within through right mental and spiritual practice. Consciousness is the inner embodiment of an idea; the subjective image of the idea; the mental and spiritual equivalent of the idea.[285]

Know your mind; train yourself to think what you wish to think; be what you wish to be; feel what you wish to feel; and do not limit yourself. After all, everything that exists in the physical realm is nothing more than mental action and reaction. If you have reached the point where your consciousness produces all things, then your thought is simply the announcement of reality.[286]

Making your mental images manifest in the physical reality may be likened to the process of dropping water into a bottle. If your thoughts are not correct, the water will also be cloudy, but right thinking means you feed pure water into the bottle, a drop at a time. It's like the formation of a stalactite. Each one begins as a single mineral-laden drop of water on the roof of a cave. When the drop falls, it leaves an almost imperceptible ring of calcite. Each subsequent drop deposits another sedimentary ring, until eventually a long, elongated tooth of rock is formed. In the same way, each thought we have is layered on top of the previous one to form our reality.[287]

Whether we believe our thoughts are the product of our minds or are mediated by the divine principle, nothing can happen or exist unless it has first been conceived of as thought.[288]

For example, let's suppose you own a shop that is struggling to attract customers. The image of your deserted shop is the image that has taken seed in your mind to become your reality. To rectify this situation, you should mentally picture the premises bustling with enthusiastic shoppers. Do this every day and tell yourself that this is what you want to happen and, through the divine mind, this visual concept you have created in your mind of a thriving business will become a reality.[289]

Nothing is real to us unless we make it real. Nothing can touch us unless we let it touch us. Refuse to let your feelings be hurt. Don't let anyone else dismiss what you are doing as useless or irrelevant. Your mind is independent, so believe and feel that you are wonderful. This is not being arrogant, this is simply the truth. What can be more wonderful than the manifestation of the infinite mind?[290]

MENTAL ATMOSPHERES

Each of us has a mental atmosphere, which is the result of everything we have ever thought, said, done and consciously or unconsciously perceived. This mental atmosphere subtly affects whether or not we are attracted to someone. Contrary to what we are led to believe, personal attraction has little to do with looks; it goes much deeper and is almost entirely subjective. This is why each of us will like and dislike different people. It also explains why, when we are out and about, we find we are drawn to certain people, with whom we feel the urge to stop and chat, yet at other times when we see someone approaching, something compels us to avoid them. Although it may seem there is no reason for us to act this way, this is the result of their mental atmosphere or thought vibration.[291]

When we come into contact with other people, we are instantly attracted or repelled, according to the vibrations we feel. A person with an atmosphere of love and generosity whose nature is to be happy and who lives an honest, wholesome life will always attract friends.[292]

Children have a heightened awareness of mental atmosphere. They will usually be drawn to those who are inwardly just and shun those who are inwardly wrong. People whom children are wary of often prove to be dangerous individuals. The same is true of animals, which have an almost entirely subjective perception of reality and feel mental atmospheres more keenly than most people can.[293]

Be what you want to attract

The philosopher Ralph Waldo Emerson wrote: "If you want a friend, be one." In other words, if you want to have friends, you should become friendly. Equally well, if you wish to find love, you should learn to love. There is no reason why anyone should not be able to possess the power of attraction, since it is a mental quality and may be consciously induced through right practice.[294]

Places can acquire atmospheres in the same way that people do. And just as a person's atmosphere is the result of their thoughts, so the atmosphere of a particular place stems from the thoughts that have been created there. These atmospheres are readily picked up by people present in that location and transmitted mentally to others.[295]

It is not just small areas and spaces that acquire an atmosphere, the same is true of entire towns, cities and even nations. Some towns, for example, bustle with life and activity while others seem dead; some are filled with a spirit of culture and creativity, while others seem possessed by a spirit of commercial greed and conflict. This is the result of the accumulated mentalities of those who live in these places. Just as a city has its own atmosphere, so too does a nation. In fact, the combined atmosphere of each of the millions of individuals living in a country is often said to create a "national mentality" or contribute to the "psychology" of its people.[296]

LIMITLESSNESS

All limits are mental

There are no limits, except for those you construct and impose on yourself. You can have anything you want, be anyone you want and do whatever you want in life. This might sound implausible – irresponsible even – if throughout your childhood and at school and work, it has been drummed into you that there are strict boundaries limiting what you can and can't do. But have you ever put this to the test? If you haven't, you should because then you will realize that this widely endorsed truth is not so true after all.

THE LAW OF ABUNDANCE

Nothing is limited. Through the law of abundance, we know that there is a spirit of infinite plenty whose power enables thoughts to manifest in material form. If you live in acceptance and in harmony with this infinite power, you will find you are able to attract a continual supply of whatever it is you desire.[297]

If you think of yourself as being poor, you will remain poor. But if you believe yourself to be prosperous, even if your present conditions suggest otherwise, you set into motion forces that will sooner or later bring you wealth. The law of attraction applies consistently throughout the universe, underpinned by the great and immutable fact that like attracts like.[298]

Like attracts Like

Your ability to attract all the things you want in life depends on the extent to which you are at one with the infinite power – the source of all things. If the relationship is harmonious and enduring, you will always be able to actualize the conditions in your life that you seek. Everything you desire exists at this present moment; it is up to you to activate the power within to bring them into your reality.[299]

The same infinite power that created and governs our solar system and the myriad of stars and planets in our universe is at work within you. Thought is a force with occult and mysterious powers, so send out your thought that the right situation, the right work, the right partner – whatever it is you seek – will come into your life at the right time, in the right way, and that you will recognize it when it arrives. Cling to this thought, never allow it to weaken, and continually water it with the strength of your conviction. By so doing, you put your advertisement into a psychical, spiritual newspaper that has an unlimited circulation; one that will make its way not only to the far-flung corners of the Earth, but to the very edges of the universe. Moreover, it is an advertisement which, if placed with goodwill on your part, will be far more effective than any ad you could ever hope to include in any earthly publication. The degree to which this will be effective, however, will depend on how thoroughly you live in harmony with the higher laws and forces.[300]

There are three things you must do in order to receive whatever it is you desire:

1) Affirm continuously your heart's desire;
2) Believe your desire will manifest in the physical world;
3) Expect that it will happen within a period of time set by you.[301]

When you see an opportunity coming up that is the manifestation of your desires, act immediately. But if this situation does not prove to be exactly what you want, and you feel you are capable of better, then realize that this situation is a stepping stone that will lead you to the opportunity that is right for you. Hold this thought doggedly, affirm it, believe it, expect it, and at all times be faithful to it.[302]

The law of abundance teaches us not to be discouraged when faced with apparent adversity. Instead, we should make the most of it and always look forward to better and more prosperous conditions. If you wholeheartedly embrace this frame of mind you will set into motion subtle, silent, and irresistible forces that sooner or later will translate your ideas into material form. Ideas have occult power and when rightly planted and rightly tended, they are the seeds that activate material conditions.[303]

Affirm whatever you desire calmly and quietly, yet firmly and confidently. **Believe** it absolutely. **Expect** it: keep your desire continually watered with expectation. In this way you will become a magnet that draws towards you the things you desire. This is the law of attraction, which, contrary to what the laws of physics have to say about magnets, makes you attract that which you wish to have.[304]

For example, let's say a young woman urgently wants money. It's for a good purpose and she sees no reason why she shouldn't have it. She comes to an understanding of the power of the interior forces and strives to adopt the frame of mind outlined above. The next morning, she enters into meditation – and in so doing she brings herself into a more complete harmony with the higher powers. Before the end of the day, a family friend phones to ask if she would be willing to do some work for his family. She's a little taken aback, but thinks to herself, I'll do it and see what it will lead to. So she takes on the work and does very well. When she is paid far more than she had expected, she protests that the sum is too large for the task she has performed. But the family stands by their decision. The sum thus received was more than sufficient for the work she wished to accomplish.[305]

This is just one example of how a connection with the higher powers can be beneficial. It also teaches us that we should not simply sit back and expect things to drop into our lap but should set in motion the higher forces and then take action.[306]

The basis for attracting the best that the world can give you is first to own and live these things in your mind – or what is often falsely called imagination. All so-called imaginings are realities that are yet to be manifested in the physical world.[307]

Absolute faith is the one immutable law of true success. When we recognize that we carry our success or our failures with us and that they do not depend on outside conditions, we attain powers that allow us to be, to do, or to have whatever we desire. When we come into this higher realization and bring our lives into complete harmony with the higher laws, we are then able to focus and direct the awakened interior forces to attract prosperity and success.[308]

DO YOU NEED EVIDENCE OF THE LAW BEFORE YOU BELIEVE IT?

Have you ever seen the law that causes a plant to grow? Of course you haven't, and yet you believe in the unseen rule of nature that decides when and how a shoot will burst from a seed and head blindly towards the sun. We accept this without question because every year this seed yields a harvest. So, why not have as great a faith in the higher laws of being? To those souls who have dared to believe has come as definite an answer as came to those who believed in receiving a harvest from the planted seed. This receiving is a mental process, a process in which we lose all sense of limitation.[309]

If you wish to demonstrate prosperity, begin to think and talk about it and to see it everywhere. Do nothing that contradicts this thought, either mentally or physically. The world is full of good – take it and let go of everything else. No living soul can demonstrate two things at the same time if one contradicts the other. Let go of all that you do not wish to become a part of your experience and, in your mind, take all that you wish.[310]

See, hear, talk about, and read only what you wish, and never let a wrong thought come into your mind.[311]

We are surrounded by a great universal thought power that always returns to us exactly what we think. This mind is so malleable and so receptive that it takes the slightest impression and moulds it into our living reality.[312]

ALL IS MIND

Everything in the universe is a product of the mind, including us. We can only get what we focus our thoughts upon. If we don't get what we desire, this is because we didn't truly believe this was achievable. Similarly, the reason others succeed is because they had complete faith they could. As a consequence, they allowed real power to flow through them and out into expression.[313]

Hold an object in front of a mirror and its reflected image will be exactly the same size as the object. If we change the object, so its reflection changes accordingly. The same is true of thought. Hold a thought in mind and it will create an exact material likeness of that thought. If we change that thought, its manifestation in the physical realm will change in exactly the same way.[314]

When we believe and affirm something will happen, we must resist the temptation to subsequently think opposite thoughts, which could serve to undermine the power of these affirmations. At times, there seems to be something in human nature that compels us to look for and find only the negative in people and situations. For example, some of us might complain that life never gives you what you want, that there aren't enough good jobs, that times are hard and prices are high, or that nobody wants what we have to offer. No one who says these sorts of things succeeds in life. When we express ourselves in this way we are using a destructive power. We must banish all such thoughts, and we must realize we play an active role at the heart of the only power there is.[315]

If you absolutely believe that you can do a certain thing, the opportunity will always present itself to you. If you believe that something cannot be done, then you are making that a law, and it will therefore not be done. Confusion brings more confusion, peace brings more peace.[316]

Virtually the entire human race is hypnotized into thinking whatever it is told to think. We derive our concept of truth from our physical environment. We look around us and we see sickness, misery, unhappiness, calamity and we feed this information into our creative mind, and by doing so we make a law for ourselves that will produce what we believe in.[317]

Like produces like, attracts like, creates like. If we could take a photograph of our thoughts, then compare it to a snapshot of the conditions in which we live, we would see no difference between the two, for they are simply the inside and outside of the same thing.[318]

We cannot make affirmations for 15 minutes a day, then spend the rest of our time denying that which we have affirmed and affirming that which we have denied, and then expect to obtain the results we seek. What we think sets the power in motion. If we then think the very opposite thing, the initial thought is neutralized and the result is... nothing.[319]

Expect that only the best things will happen to you. Be content and cheerful if you wish to attract from the store of the infinite – don't sit around waiting for trouble. Open up your whole consciousness to the greater possibilities of life. Align yourself with all that is significant and meaningful.[320]

EXPANDING OUR THOUGHT

All things come to us through the use of thought. If we have a small, limited concept of life, we will always be doing small, insignificant things. Unless we are constantly expanding our thought, we are not growing. Growth is one of the fundamental laws of life and it is essential we embrace it. We cannot stand still. If you want to do a new thing, get a new thought and then you will activate the power of attraction that will help draw towards you circumstances that will help you to achieve your goal. Reject poisonous concepts that limit you.[321]

Do not be afraid either to break free from thoughts that have ruled you in the past. Set yourself a new agenda. If you want to own your own restaurant, you will never do it unless you get beyond the idea that the most you can hope for in life is to flip burgers. It's OK for people who work behind the counter at a fast food restaurant to think about flipping burgers, but if you aspire to something else, then train your thoughts on this goal.[322]

SIMPLE RULES FOR PROSPERITY

Here are a few simple rules for attracting prosperity into your life. Remember that nothing happens by chance. All is law and all is order. You create your own laws every time you think. There is a powerful energy all around you that knows and understands everything. This power works like the soil: as soon as it receives the seed of your thought it starts bringing its influence to bear, encouraging your thoughts to germinate and blossom into reality. It will receive whatever you give to it and will create for you and throw back at you whatever you think into it.[323]

Thought can attract to us only that which we first mentally embody. We cannot attract to ourselves that which we are not. We can attract in the outer only that which has first become a part of our mental DNA – a part of our inner understanding.[324]

A man running his own business will attract whatever he thinks about the most. If he is a barber, he will attract people who want to be shaved or who need a haircut. If he sells shoes, he will attract people who need new shoes. This rule applies to anything we think about and put our mind to. We will always attract as much of anything as we mentally embody. It is not enough to say that we attract what we think – we become what we think, and what we become we will attract.[325]

To conclude, all we need to do is to free our minds from any limitations imposed on us by others and by ourselves during our lives. And by now, we have learnt how to achieve this on a conscious and subconscious level.

September - Happiness

Happiness is the meaning and the purpose of life, the whole aim and end of human existence.[326]

ARISTOTLE

WHAT IS HAPPINESS

According to the Cambridge Dictionary, happiness is "the feeling of being happy". Happy, according to the same source, means "feeling, showing or causing pleasure or satisfaction".[327]

Wikipedia goes even further, defining happiness as "a state of mind or feeling characterized by contentment, love, satisfaction, pleasure, or joy"[328]. Wikipedia is a great site, written for the people by the people. So let's see what a few of them have to say about happiness.

In October 2008, *Psychology Today*[329] asked people on the streets of New York what makes them happy. The results were revealing. One person responded by saying, "When I'm worried about something, I go shopping. I always feel great when I have new things." Another said, "I'm always happy. That's my style. I always rely on my friends. If anything bad does happen, I go swimming or skateboarding or surfing." Another passerby, clearly anticipating a victory for the Democrat candidate in the forthcoming Presidential election, said, "I'll be happy when Barack Obama wins. He's changing the world. The improvement in the economy and healthcare make me a happier woman".

I love New York and New Yorkers, but the people questioned above do not strike me as particularly happy. What they do show is an ability to master external contentment methods and a "pursuit of happiness" mentality.

HAPPINESS VS WEALTH

Does money make us happy? Economists have long argued that richer nations tend to be happier than poorer nations – a view supported by recent research by the World Economic Forum that found higher GDP (gross domestic product: the total products and services produced by a nation) usually means better education, lower child mortality, a better lifestyle and, consequently, a measurably happier population.[330]

The problem with this viewpoint, however, is that there is a limit to how much longevity, literacy and good health money can buy. Studies suggest that beyond an average GDP/capita of about $15,000 a year, income makes little difference to the average happiness of the population.[331] In fact, if you were to measure the increased levels of happiness that cash alone can achieve, the upwardly arcing curve would eventually become a straight line.[332]

THE HAPPIEST PLACE IN THE WORLD[333]

Which do you think is the happiest country in the world? You may be surprised to learn that a report published by UK advisory body, the Sustainable Development Commission, concluded that when levels of sustainability and wellbeing are compared internationally, the number one nation is… Costa Rica.[334]

The report, *Prosperity Without Growth*, used a formula devised by independent British think-tank the New Economics Foundation (NEF), called the Happy Planet Index (HPI). This measures the degree to which long and happy lives (life satisfaction and life expectancy are multiplied together to calculate "happy life years") are achieved per unit of environmental impact.[335]

The highest life expectancies tend to be in rich, developed countries. Western Europe, North America, Japan, Hong Kong and Australasia are among the leaders, while Africa lags far behind with a very low life expectancy.[336]

The next component of the formula is life satisfaction. This is calculated by asking people: "How satisfied are you with your life as a whole these days?"[337]

At first glance, it appears that rich Western countries dominate again, but closer inspection reveals that almost a third of the top 35 countries have a GDP per capita of less than $20,000. According to the NEF, "the country with the highest reported life satisfaction – and by some margin – is Costa Rica (8.5 on a scale of 0-10, compared with 8.1 for Ireland, Norway and Denmark)".[338]

The final element of the HPI score is based on the size of a country's ecological footprint. The report explains the thinking like this: "To achieve one-planet living, a country must keep its ecological footprint below the level that corresponds to its fair share given the world's current biocapacity and population – 2.1 global hectares (gha) in 2005." Therefore, a country with a score of 2.1 achieves one-planet living. Anything over 4.2 is two-planet living, and so on. Inevitably, rich, consumer societies fare badly when judged using this criteria.[339]

The countries with the smallest per capita footprints are among the poorest: Malawi, Haiti and Bangladesh. The countries with the biggest ecological footprints are Luxembourg (10.2 gha), the United Arab Emirates (9.5 gha) and the US (9.4 gha) – all of which consume four times their fair share of global resources. Interestingly, the Netherlands achieves the same level of happy life years as the US, but with a footprint less than half its size (4.4 gha).[340]

After all the math has been done, not only does Costa Rica come out top, but nine of the top ten countries in the HPI are in Latin America and the Caribbean.

The researchers conclude: "Latin Americans report being much less concerned with material issues than, for example, they are with their friends and family. Civil society is very active – from religious groups to workers' groups to environmental groups. Some have mocked the high levels of reported life satisfaction in Latin American countries as belying a lack of knowledge of anything better (i.e. Western lifestyles). On the contrary, Latin America is perhaps more exposed to North American culture than anywhere else in the developing world. Yet somehow it has been more resistant to idolizing this lifestyle, or at least more able to be happy with its own way of life despite this influence. "Pura vida" is a popular expression in Costa Rica and is used somewhat like the English term "cool". It translates literally as "pure life" and represents in itself an attitude to what is important."[341]

So, happiness is not all about having lots of money. Could this mean that religion holds the key instead?

HAPPINESS IN RELIGIOUS MOVEMENTS[342]

According to Catholicism, the ultimate goal of human existence is "blessed happiness" – being grateful and appreciating God's creation.[343]

A recent study presented to the Royal Economic Society conference in Britain claimed that religious people are better able to cope with extremely stressful or traumatic events, such as losing a job or divorce. The research found that among the thousands of Europeans it polled, "life satisfaction" was higher for believers than for non-believers.[344]

This is not the first study to draw links between religion and happiness.[345] For example, Professor Clark, from the Paris School of Economics, and co-author Dr Orsolya Lelkes, from the European Center for Social Welfare Policy and Research, used information from household surveys to analyse the attitudes of Christians – both Catholic and Protestant – not only to their own happiness, but also on issues such as unemployment. Their findings, they said, suggest that for many people religion serves as a "buffer" to protect them from life's disappointments.[346]

Professor Clark said: "We originally started the research to work out why some European countries had more generous unemployment benefits than others, but our analysis suggested that religious people suffered less psychological harm from unemployment than the non-religious. They had higher levels of life satisfaction".[347]

Happiness is a central theme in Buddhist teachings. For ultimate freedom from suffering, the Eightfold Path – the fourth of Buddha's Noble Truths – leads followers to Nirvana, a state of everlasting peace. Accordingly, ultimate happiness is only achieved by overcoming craving in all forms. More mundane forms of happiness, such as acquiring wealth and maintaining friendships, are also recognized as worthy goals. Buddhism also encourages loving kindness and compassion. According to the Buddha, "Mind is the forerunner of states of existence. Mind is chief, and those states are caused by the mind. If one speaks and acts with a pure mind, surely happiness will follow like one's own shadow." In Buddhism, the third of the Four Noble Truths says, "to eliminate suffering, eliminate craving". In other words, happiness transcends material and emotional possession and is attainable only by striving to eliminate uncontrollable urges.[348]

Those two great belief systems hint at where true happiness lies. Through Catholicism we can conclude that gratitude is a gateway to happiness, whereas Buddhism urges us to go further and to look into ourselves. Shall we?

WHERE DOES HAPPINESS COME FROM?

Those who try to find their love and happiness in possessions, places or people are destined to be miserable because they fail to understand that true happiness can only be found within themselves. Everlasting joy, happiness and love all come from falling in love with yourself. The people, places and things that you attract into your life that make you happy only serve to enhance the love that you already have for yourself. They can never replace that inner love. If you seek true happiness, practice giving unconditional love – and the first person you must show true love to is yourself (see January – Self-Love).[349]

We are all searching for happiness. Although this means something different for each of us, most of us seem to think that it can only be found outside of ourselves. We typically might say: "When I move house, things will be better"; "When I have enough money, things will be OK"; "When I change jobs, I'll be happier"; "When I am not so stressed, my life will be much better", etc.[350]

Consider this cautionary tale: One day, a very old woman was walking along the road when a stranger carrying a bag stopped and asked her how far the nearest town was. When she told him, he asked her, "What kind of town is it to live in?" The old woman replied, "What kind of town are you from?" The stranger replied, "Oh, its awful: people are critical of each other, it's not very neighborly, no one helps anyone and people are generally miserable. I'm glad to be leaving." "Well," said the old woman, "I am very sorry to have to tell you that's exactly what it's like where you are going."[351]

A while later, the old lady passed another stranger who stopped to ask her how far it was to the nearest town. She told him and then he asked, "What kind of town is it to live in?" The old woman replied, "What kind of town are you from?" The stranger answered, "It's a great place, people are kind and helpful, and I have made some good friends and wherever you go there is always a welcome and a smile; I am sad to be leaving." "Well," said the old woman, "I am pleased to tell you that is exactly what it is like where you are headed."[352]

The moral of this story is that no matter where you live, your attitude alone will determine whether it is a horrible or a wonderful place.[353]

Around 2,500 years ago, the Chinese philosopher Lao Tzu said: "The biggest problem in the world is that individuals experience themselves as powerless." Today, this is still our biggest problem. The main barrier to happiness and success is our feeling of powerlessness, which causes negativity, anger, anxiety, inertia and fear.[354]

Personal power comes from an inner sense of security, which is achieved by knowing who you are, connecting your thoughts and feelings with your inner self, and then accepting yourself. By accepting yourself, you can be yourself and other people's opinions and criticisms cannot make you feel so insecure that you feel worthlessness. Personal Power comes from within; no one can give it to you.[355]

Retaining your power requires you to take control of your thinking. This way, you alone decide how you think, which in turn affects how you feel, how you behave and what your attitude is. Take care of yourself;

look after your physical, emotional health and spiritual needs. Let no one else be in charge of your life but you.[356]

You cannot change how others relate to the world, or how they relate to you. However, you can change yourself. Look closely at what blocks your inner vision and you will be amazed how quickly the fog disappears and a clear, focused picture emerges.[357]

THE PURSUIT OF HAPPINESS

A lot has been written and said about the pursuit of happiness. In 1776, the US Declaration of Independence enshrined in law the inalienable human rights of every American citizen. Among these was the freedom to pursue happiness. What an irony. If you "pursue" happiness, the last thing you are is "free". Instead, you will always be a prisoner, destined to forever be chasing something that remains beyond your reach. You cannot pursue happiness any more than you can rely on someone else to make you happy. The only way to be happy is to be happy, right *now*.

HAPPINESS COMES FROM WITHIN

Happiness, like unhappiness, is a product of our minds – even though we often project those feelings outwards, insisting that the world at large is responsible for our state of mind. Since the causes of happiness and unhappiness reside within us, ultimately they are within our control – we can choose whether to be happy or not.

Happiness is inside us and is attainable[358]

When the clouds hide the sun, the sun is still there. Like the clouds, thoughts, worries and desires can cover and hide our happiness. We have to disperse them in order to experience it. Then the inherent and ever-lasting happiness in the soul can shine forth.[359]

Happiness is not something far away and unattainable and it does not depend on external circumstances. Objects and events are not its causes; it is an inseparable part of our consciousness. But as mentioned earlier, it is hidden and covered from sight by the endless procession of thoughts, desires and worries in our minds.[360]

The experience of mystics through the ages has been that happiness is inherent in our souls. But to find it, our minds must first be calm and relaxed, free from the chatter of our thoughts.[361]

All the mystics, yogis and saints in history have not been searching for pleasure, but for an inextinguishable inner happiness that exists independently from everything outside of us. Such happiness is constant and eternal and part of our nature; only our thoughts can stand in the way of us experiencing it. Banish these thoughts and happiness is attainable.[362]

You cannot see treasure lying on the bed of a storm-tossed sea, but it is there. Make the water still, let the sediment settle to the ocean floor, and the treasure will reveal itself to you. So it is with happiness; it is always here, only covered and hidden.[363]

You may wonder what you have to do to gain happiness, but it is already there within you. Just calm your mind and stay relaxed and you will experience it. There is no need to wait for circumstances and events to bring it to you. A calm and detached mind is the gateway to true happiness. It is your decision to choose happiness; happiness is inside you. This advice has been communicated to us down the ages:[364]

1. You choose

Most people are about as happy as they make up their minds to be.
Abraham Lincoln

Very little is needed to make a happy life; it is all within yourself, in your way of thinking.
Marcus Aurelius Antoninus

The world of those who are happy is different from the world of those who are not.
Ludwig Wittgenstein

The world around you is filtered through the lens of your senses. Depending on whether you interpret this information in a positive or a negative way, you will either find happiness in small, everyday things or blame the circumstances of your life for your lack of contentment. Your choices control the levels of happiness in your life.

Strive to be detached, and don't let your feelings be influenced by trivial matters. If you convince yourself to stay relaxed and calm in every situation, then you have chosen happiness. Activities such as meditation (see October – Awareness) will train your mind to stay focused and calm, and will help you develop willpower and self-discipline. Such disciplines are the gateway to happiness.

2. Focus on the present, not yesterday or tomorrow

When one door of happiness closes another opens, but often we look so long at the closed door that we do not see the one that has been opened for us.
Helen Keller

The foolish man seeks happiness in the distance; the wise grows it under his feet.
James Oppenheim

Yesterday is history, tomorrow is a mystery, today is God's gift, that's why we call it the present.
Joan Rivers

You only have now … and now … and now. Yesterday is a memory that you cannot change. Tomorrow is merely a fantasy that exists in your mind right now. So live more in the now by focusing on the present moment and today. If you think and worry too much about yesterday and tomorrow, you risk missing out on a great deal of happiness that is available to you right now.

3. Be grateful

Man is fond of counting his troubles, but he does not count his joys. If he counted them up as he ought to, he would see that every lot has enough happiness provided for it.
Fyodor Dostoevsky

We tend to forget that happiness doesn't come as a result of getting something we don't have, but rather of recognizing and appreciating what we do have.
Frederick Keonig

Let us be grateful to people who make us happy; they are the charming gardeners who make our souls blossom.
Marcel Proust

One of the simplest and quickest ways to turn a negative and sour mood into a more positive one is to be grateful (see November – Gratitude).

Among the many things you can feel gratitude for are the sunshine and the weather, the roof over your head, your health, a good TV show, a movie or a song, your friends, family, work colleagues, and the people you meet walking down the street.

Just for a minute, try feeling grateful for these things and see how it changes how you feel – it's a win-win situation! You feel great because you are grateful about your world, and the people you are grateful for feel great too because they feel appreciated. So don't forget about gratitude or you may forget about the happiness that already exists in your life.

4. Help someone else find happiness

Since you get more joy out of giving joy to others, you should put a good deal of thought into the happiness that you are able to give.
Eleanor Roosevelt

Thousands of candles can be lighted from a single candle, and the life of the candle will not be shortened. Happiness never decreases by being shared.
Buddha

If you want happiness for an hour – take a nap.
If you want happiness for a day – go fishing.
If you want happiness for a year – inherit a fortune.
If you want happiness for a lifetime – help someone else.
Chinese Proverb

Happiness is like a kiss. You must share it to enjoy it.
Bernard Meltzer

When you make someone else happy – by, for example, helping them with something – you can sense, see, feel and hear it, and that happy feeling flows back to you. And then, if you choose to, you can boost you own ego by thinking something like: "Wow, I really made him/her happy!"

And because the law of reciprocity is so strong, there is another upside: people will feel like giving back to you. Or they might feel like helping or sharing it with someone else. And so the two – or more – of you keep spreading the happiness.

In the East, it is said that if you are in the presence of a renowned teacher, your thoughts slow down and you experience elation and bliss. The mind of such a teacher is completely calm and undisturbed by thought, allowing happiness to flourish around them without obstacle. It is also very powerful and can cause the minds of people nearby to behave similarly, as though influenced by telepathy.

5. Do what you like doing

Success is not the key to happiness. Happiness is the key to success. If you love what you are doing, you will be successful.
Albert Schweitzer

Happiness is not in the mere possession of money; it lies in the joy of achievement, in the thrill of creative effort.
Franklin D. Roosevelt

It's very easy to let yourself get stuck doing things you don't want to do for hours on end, never making time to do what you really love doing. While you might not be able to do what you want to do right now, you almost always have a choice to do more of what you really want to do. There is always time. Or time you can free up. You have a choice.

6. Or at least do something

Action may not always bring happiness; but there is no happiness without action.
Benjamin Disraeli

Twenty years from now you will be more disappointed by the things that you didn't do than by the ones you did do.
So throw off the bowlines. Sail away from the safe harbor. Catch the trade winds in your sails. Explore. Dream. Discover.
Mark Twain

One of the best ways to not find happiness is to sit back and do nothing, or paralyse yourself through over-analysis. It's not always easy to be proactive. In fact, it can be scary and difficult at times. But if you don't seize the moment, you risk missing out on a lot, including moments, people and experiences that can bring you a lot of happiness.

SPREADING HAPPINESS

Have you ever noticed how happiness is contagious? The way this works is actually quite simple. Let's say that one day you're feeling particularly gloomy. You go into a grocery store and the shop assistant greets you by saying, "Good morning! What a wonderful dress/suit you're wearing." or "You have the most beautiful eyes!" A few warm words of encouragement like this from another person can trigger positive feelings inside you that may prompt you to do something similar for someone else a short while later, such as helping an old lady cross the street.

You can be the one who instigates this chain of events. Each time, think of something nice to tell another person. Even a simple hello or a smile can help change someone else's day for the better. And when you do this, you will see how other people will reflect the happiness and enthusiasm you have shown them back to you.

While concluding my research for this book, I spoke enthusiastically about my project with my friend Agnieszka. She shared the excitement and joy I was feeling about my work and very soon started to become similarly enthused about a project of her own that she had long kept on the back burner. We were like two mirrors reflecting excitement and happiness back at each other and cumulating this feeling of joy.

However, this happiness was not only a mutual phenomenon, we were spreading it far and wide. We were happy and other people who spent time with us also became happy. One time, while having a coffee with another friend of mine, she stared at me and smiled. When I asked her why she was smiling, she told me that just by looking at me she had started to feel happy. This encounter shows that when you are truly joyful, it's contagious – like a cold you would want to catch!

FINAL THOUGHT

All the things you choose to do are intended to help you get to a happy place. So, why not just take a short cut and start being happy in yourself right now?[365]

Happiness is always within us. Even when the sky is cloudy, the sun is still behind the clouds. Even when our minds are cluttered, our happiness is there to be found, waiting for us to cast aside the clutter and look within.

October Again – Celebration Day

A year and a day have passed and an amazing adventure is reaching a milestone. The end – of the beginning. A reason to celebrate. I believe that mastering your thoughts is the true path to happiness and anything you desire. I hold this belief, not because wise people said it. I hold this belief, not because in some traditions it is generally held. I hold this belief, not because it is said in ancient books. I hold this belief, not because it is said to be of divine origin. I hold this belief, not because many others believe this. I hold this belief because I myself tested it and judged to be true.

I am aware of who I am and what I am doing here. I am grateful for this wonderful experience, I am full of unconditional love and I desire to demonstrate that any limits you might impose on yourself are merely the limits of your own mind. In reality, there are no limits.

I believe in celebrations. They give you a sense of accomplishment, they give you the opportunity to step aside from whatever it is you're doing for a while, smile with contentment, pat yourself on the shoulder and think: "Wow – this sure is something." In this particular moment, you are grateful to the universe and you are grateful to yourself. You know you are invincible and you know this celebration is both an end and a beginning. It's the end of a series of endeavors and the beginning of a new journey, which will be built on this one.

Let's celebrate this with a special meditation session.

EXERCISE 24: CELEBRATION MEDITATION

Prepare the perfect surroundings. If it feels right, dim the lights and light candles – choose the colors to suit the major theme of your meditation. I choose white for a clear mind, calling in positive and serene energy; pink for self-love, happiness and joy in life; red for passion and personal empowerment; green for wealth; yellow for wisdom; orange for youth, beauty and completion; and purple for health and enhancing my magical powers.

Choose the right music – something that will enhance the majesty of the situation. And choose the right clothing. The best place and time will be one that suits you best, but I suggest you stick to the place and time you have used so far for your mental works. Make sure you won't be disturbed.

Bring yourself to a meditative state. From now on, you are officially a conscious magician of life. In a meditative state, say on an inhale-exhale basis: **"I am a conscious magician of life",** *concentrating on the candle colors representing the qualities you are. Repeat* **"I am love, I am joy, I am wealth, I am health, I am youth, I am peace, I am beauty, I am wisdom, I am power".** *Do it as long as you need in order to be fully attuned with this energy. Say:* **"I am divine perfection, I am aware of my power of creation and I am grateful for it. I bless all the people and things I come into contact with, clearly spreading love, joy and peace, wherever I go.** *(I bless this book and all the people who will read it to fully experience their divinity and attain enlightenment)".* *Feel all the colors from the candles form a colorful sphere around you and know that they will be there always as an integral part of your aura.*

When you fully feel your divine perfection and your purpose, celebrate! Perform a joyful dance of gratitude for all the spiritual growth of the last year. Celebrate all the wisdom you have acquired. Alternatively, perform a song of gratitude, or play a musical instrument, or make a drawing, or write a poem – release your creativity, express your joy to the universe.

Cakes & Ale
Now you need to get back from the magical world, bringing your magical self to the reality we live in. Ground yourself with the traditional "Cakes & Ale".

Postscript

Life is meant to be lived in eternal bliss, infinite freedom, unconditional love and unbounded awareness. Any other life is utterly missing the point of being born a human.[366]

MSI

Bibliography

Abraham-Hicks. (1999) Excerpted from the workshop in Portland, OR on Sunday, July 11th. *In:* Personal Development Forum. Available at: http://www.personaldevelopmentforum.com/abraham-hicks.html [Accessed 24 March 2010].

Abraham-Hicks. (2002) Excerpted from the workshop in El Paso, TX on Thursday, March 28th. *In:* Gaia Community. Available at: http://www.gaia.com/quotes/abraham_hicks [Accessed 24 March 2010].

Abraham-Hicks. (2004) Excerpted from the workshop in Washington, DC on Saturday, May 1st.

Abraham-Hicks. (2005) Excerpted from the workshop in Washington, DC on Saturday, May 7th. *In:* Gaia Community. Available at: http://www.gaia.com/quotes/abraham_hicks [Accessed 24 March 2010].

ACFNewSource (2006) Gratitude Theory. Available at: http://www.acfnewsource.org/religion/gratitude_theory.html [Accessed 20 March 2010].

Aristotle. *In:* ThinkExist. Available at: http://thinkexist.com/quotation/happiness_is_the_meaning_and_the_purpose_of_life/171697.html [Accessed 26 March 2010].

Atkinson, W. W. (2008, first published 1918) *The Secret Doctrine of the Rosicrucians.* Forgotten Books. Available at: http://books.google.com/books/p/pub-4297897631756504?id=RIrhC_vEHXAC&printsec=frontcover&dq=The+Secret+Doctrine+of+the+Rosicrucian&ei=fvSpS8bzJZ2uMov0tbYM&cd=1#v=onepage&q=The%20Secret%20Doctrine%20of%20the%20Rosicrucian&f=false [Accessed 24 March 2010].

Aubrey, A. (2005) Science Explores Meditation's Effect on Brain. Available at: http://www.npr.org/templates/story/story.php?storyId=4770779 [Accessed 20 March 2010].

Baer, G. (2009) What is Real Love? Real Love. Available at: http://www.reallove.com/about.asp [Accessed 22 March 2010].

Barbor, C. (2001) The Science of Meditation. *Psychology Today*. Available at: http://www.psychologytoday.com/articles/200105/the-science-meditation [Accessed 20 March 2010].

Beattie, M. (2007) *Gratitude*. Minnesota, Hazelden Foundation.

Bermeitinger, C. *et al* (2009) The hidden persuaders break into the tired brain. *Journal of Experimental Social Psychology, 45,* pp320-326.

Bourbeau, L. (2001) *Your Body's Telling You: Love Yourself! The most complete book on metaphysical causes of illnesses & diseases.* Quebec, Les Editions E.T.C. Inc.

Brother Veritus, The Art and Science of Unconditional Love. Unconditional Love. Available at: http://www.luisprada.com/Protected/Unconditional_Love.htm [Accessed 22 March 2010].

Buckland, R. (2002) *Buckland's Complete Book of Witchcraft* ©. 2143 Wooddale Drive, Woodbury, MN 55125-2989. Llewellyn Worldwide, Ltd.

Buddha. *In:* ThinkExist. Available at: http://thinkexist.com/quotation/every_human_being_is_the_author_of_his_own_health/200690.html [Accessed 26 March 2010].

Buddha. *In:* ThinkExist. Available at: http://thinkexist.com/quotation/let_us_rise_up_and_be_thankful-for_if_we_didn-t/199980.html [Accessed 30 March 2010].

Burke, C. (2006) The Inner-Power Emails. Life with Confidence. Available at: http://www.life-with-confidence.com/support-files/inner_power_emails.pdf [Accessed 21 March 2010].

Byrne, D. (1959). The effect of a subliminal food stimulus on verbal responses. *Journal of Applied Psychology, 43*, pp249–252.

Byron, B. G. and Marchand, L. A. (1975) *Wedlock's the devil: 1814-1815*. United States, s.n.

Caesar, V. and Caesar, C.A. (2006) *The High Achiever's Guide to Happiness*. California, Corwin Press.

Cambridge Advanced Learner's Dictionary (2010) Available at: http://dictionary.cambridge.org/ [Accessed 26 March 2010].

Canfield, J. and Hansen, M. V. (1995) *A 2nd Helping of Chicken Soup for the Soul: 101 More Stories to Open the Heart and Rekindle the Spirit*. Florida, Health Communications.

Canfield, J. and Watkins, D. D. (2007) *Gratitude – A Daily Journal. Honor and Appreciate the Abundance in Your Life*. Florida, Health Communications.

Carberry, S. (2005) Chakra Balancing Visualization Exercise. The Body Mind and Soul. Available at: http://www.thebodymindandsoul.com/chakra-balancing-guided-meditation-exercise.htm [Accessed 24 March 2010].

Carter-Scott, C. (1999) *If Love is a Game, These Are the Rules*. New York, Random House.

Colby, A. (2007) Do You Love Yourself? Self Growth. Available at: http://www.selfgrowth.com/articles/Do_You_Love_Yourself.html [Accessed 22 March 2010].

Conan Doyle, A. (2010) A Scandal in Bohemia. *In: The Adventures of Sherlock Holmes*. CreateSpace.

Corbin, K. (2007) The Magic of Self-Love. EzineArticles. Available at: http://ezinearticles.com/?The-Magic-of-Self-Love&id=749500 [Accessed 22 March 2010].

DavidIcke Forum (2010) Available at: http://www.davidicke.com/forum/showthread.php?p=1058648861 [Accessed 26 March 2010].

De Angeles, L. (2008) *Witchcraft: Theory and Practice.* Woodbury, Llewellyn Publications.

Democrats smell campaign rat (2010) BBC News of 12th Sept. Available at: http://news.bbc.co.uk/2/hi/in_depth/americas/2000/us_elections/election_news/921830.stm [Accessed 26 March 2010].

Dr Quantum – Double Slit Experiment (2010). BBC5.TV. Available at: http://news.bbc5.tv/story/dr-quantum-double-slit-experiment [Accessed 23 March 2010].

Dr Seuss (1959) *Happy Birthday to You!* Party Edition. New York, Random House.

Demarco, S. (2006) *Witch in the Bedroom.* Woodbury, Llewellyn Publications.

Disney recalls video over 'nude image' (1999) BBC News of Jan 9th Available at: http://news.bbc.co.uk/2/hi/entertainment/251532.stm [Accessed 26 March 2010].

Easton, M. (2009) Map of The Week: Why Costa Rica is the happiest place. BBC of 4 July. Available at: http://www.bbc.co.uk/blogs/thereporters/markeaston/2009/07/map_of_the_week_why_costa_rica.html [Accessed 26 March 2010].

Edberg, H. (2007) How to Find Happiness: 7 Timeless Tips from the last 2500 Years. Available at: http://www.positivityblog.com/index.php/2007/09/26/how-to-find-happiness/ [Accessed 26 March 2010].

Einstein, A. *In:* ThinkExist. Available at: http://thinkexist.com/quotation/reality_is_merely_an_illusion-albeit_a_very/15556.html [Accessed 23 March 2010].

Emmons, R. A. (2007) *Thanks! How the New Science of Gratitude Can Make You Happier.* New York, Houghton-Mifflin.

Emmons, R. A. and McCullough M. E. (2003) Counting blessings versus burdens: An experimental investigation of gratitude and subjective well-being in daily life. *Journal of Personality and Social Psychology.*

Emmons, R. A. and McCullough, M. E. (2004) *The Psychology of Gratitude.* New York, Oxford University Press.

Emoto, M. (2003) *The True Power of Water. Healing And Discovering Ourselves.* New York, Atria Books.

Emoto, M. (2005) *The Hidden Messages in Water.* New York, Atria Books.

Emoto, M. (2007) *The Miracle of Water.* New York, Atria Books.

Emoto, M. (200?)*The Message from Water. Children's Book.* Emoto Peace Project. Available at: http://emotoproject.org [Accessed 22 March 2010].

EOC Institute (200?) Instant Deep Meditation. Available at: http://www.eocinstitute.org/brainwave_synchronization_s/47.htm [Accessed 20 March 2010].

Flood, G. D. (1996) *An Introduction to Hinduism.* New York, Cambridge University Press.

Flora, C. (2009) The Pursuit of Happiness. *Psychology Today, Feb.*

Fredrickson, B.L. *et al* (2003) What good are positive emotions in crises?: A prospective study of resilience and emotions following terrorist attacks on the United States in September 11, 2001. *Journal of Personality and Social Psychology*.

Freud, S. *In*: QuotationsBook. Available at: http://quotationsbook.com/quote/26442/ [Accessed 26 March 2010].

Frey, B. S. and Stutzer, A. (Dec 2001). *Happiness and Economics*. Princeton University Press.

Goddard, N. L. (ed) (2005) *The Power of Awareness*. Camarillo, CA: DeVorss & Company.

Gold, T. (2003) *What is Love?: A Simple Buddhist Guide to Romantic Happiness*. Singapore, Lionstead Press.

Gray, P. *et al* (1993) What is Love? *Time Magazine*, 15 February. Available at: http://www.time.com/time/magazine/article/0,9171,977763,00.html [Accessed 22 March 2010].

Greenwald A. *et al* (1991). Double-Blind Test of Subliminal Self-Help Audtiotapes. *American Psychological Society, 2, no. 2*.

Guthrie, G. P. (2003) *1,600 Quotes & Pieces of Wisdom That Just Might Help You Out When You're Stuck in a Moment (and can't get out of it!)*. Nebraska, iUniverse.

Hamblin, H. T. (2008, first published 1923) *Dynamic Thought: Harmony, Health, Success, Achievement*. Forgotten Books. Available at: http://books.google.com/books/p/pub-4297897631756504?id=w5uXOSU2rMkC&printsec=frontcover&dq=Dynamic+Thought:+Harmony,+Health,+Success,+Achievement&ei=BeeoS465F420MN3eraYM&hl=it&cd=1#v=onepage&q=&f=false [Accessed 23 March 2010].

Hendrick, C. and Hendrick, S. (1986) A theory and method of love. *Journal of Personality and Social Psychology, 50,* February.

Hill, N. (2008, first published 1938) *Think and Grow Rich*. Forgotten Books. Available at: http://books.google.com/books/p/

pub-4297897631756504?id=c86H36mgiM4C&printsec=frontcover
&dq=Think+and+Grow+Rich&ei=h76sS7a_L4TANpillcwM&hl=it&
cd=I#v=onepage&q=&f=false [Accessed 26 March 2010].

Holmes, E. S. (2008, first published 1926) *The Science of Mind.*
Forgotten Books. Available at: http://books.google.com/books/p/
pub-4297897631756504?id=Y45W8kh25FMC&printsec=frontcove
r&dq=The+Science+of+Mind&ei=4rusS5XyGpSoNtTApboM&cd=I
#v=onepage&q=&f=false [Accessed 26 March 2010].

Holmes, O. W. *In:* ThinkExist. Available at: http://thinkexist.com/
quotation/man-s_mind-once_stretched_by_a_new_idea-
never/8182.html [Accessed 30 March 2010].

Hughes, D. (200?) Meditation and Spirituality: An interview with
Deepak Chopra. Share Guide. Available at: http://www.shareguide.
com/Chopra2.html [Accessed 20 March 2010].

Icke, D. (1996) *I am me, I am free: The Robot's Guide to Freedom.* Bridge
of Love.

Icke, D. (2005) *Infinite Love is The Only Truth, Everything Else is Illusion.
Exposing the dreamworld we believe to be "real".* S.n.

Isha. (2008) *Why Walk When You Can Fly? Soar Beyond Your Fears and Love
Yourself and Others Unconditionally.* California, New World Library.

Karremans, J.C. *et al* (2006) Beyond Vicary's fantasies: The impact of
subliminal priming and brand choice. *Journal of Experimental Social
Psychology, 42,* pp792-798.

Key, W. B. (1973) *Subliminal seduction: Ad media's manipulation of a not so
innocent America.* Englewood Cliffs, NJ, Prentice-Hall.

Keyes, K. (1993) *The Power of Unconditional Love: 21 Guidelines for
Beginning, Improving and Changing your Most Meaningful Relationships.*
Love Line Books.

King, J. D. (2009) *World Transformation: A Guide to Personal Growth and Consciousness.* AuthorHouse UK Ltd.

King, S. K. (2003) *The Little Pink Booklet of Aloha.* Hawaii, Aloha International.

Kirtikar, M. (2006) Energy and Vibration. Available at: http://ezinearticles.com/?Energy-and-Vibration&id=356857 [Accessed 24 March 2010].

Koyre, A. (2008, first published 1913) *Mahanirvana Tantra: Tantra of the Great Liberation.* Forgotten Books. Available at: http://books.google.com/books/p/pub-4297897631756504?id=FYaIQbFtPmYC&printsec=frontcover&dq=Mahanirvana+Tantra:+Tantra+of+the+Great+Liberation&ei=LPapS4y9O4ruNMeF4awM&hl=it&cd=1#v=onepage&q=&f=false [Accessed 24 March 2010].

Kristeller, P. O. (1980). *Renaissance Thought and the Arts: Collected Essays.* Princeton University Press.

Krosnick, J. A. *et al* (1992). Subliminal Conditioning of Attitudes. *Personality and Social Psychology Bulletin, 18: 152.*

Larson, C. D. (2008, first published 1912) *Your Forces and How to Use Them.* Forgotten Books. Available at: http://books.google.com/books/p/pub-4297897631756504?id=Q6UgNYpIHigC&printsec=frontcover&dq=Your+Forces+and+How+to+Use+Them&ei=OOaoS9SsGZWQMoCmycYM&hl=it&cd=1#v=onepage&q=&f=false [Accessed 23 March 2010].

Lee, J. (1973) *Colors of Love: An Exploration of the Ways of Loving.* New York, New Press.

Loo, T. (2006) The Power of Giving Unconditional Love. EzineArticles. Available at: http://ezinearticles.com/?The-Power-of-Giving-Unconditional-Love&id=368427 [Accessed 22 March 2010].

Loo, T. (2006) The Power of Unconditional Love. Available at: http://www.selfgrowth.com/articles/TristanLoo7.html [Accessed 26 March 2010].

Lynch, C. and Daniels, V. (2000) Patterns of Relationships. Available at: http://www.sonoma.edu/users/d/daniels/lynch.html [Accessed 23 March 2010].

Lyubomirsky, S. (2007) *The How of Happiness. A New Approach to Getting the Life You Want.* United States, Penguin Books.

Maharishi Sadashiva Isham. *In:* Find-happiness. Available at: http://www.find-happiness.com/benefits-of-meditation.html [Accessed 11 April 2010].

Maine, M. (2005) 20 Ways to Love Your Body!! National Eating Disorders Association. Available at http://www.nationaleatingdisorders.org/nedaDir/files/documents/handouts/20WaysTo.pdf [Accessed 22 March 2010].

Manahan, R. (2007) The Power of the Written Word. Fortify Your Oasis. Available at: http://fortifyservices.blogspot.com/2007/06/power-of-written-word.html [Accessed 21 March 2010].

Mascaró, J. (2003). *The Bhagavad Gita.* New York, Penguin Classics.

Mauchline, P. (200?) The Perfect Partner. Available at www.artofloving.com [Accessed 22 March 2010].

McGrath, E. (2002) The Power of Love. *Psychology Today.* Available at: http://www.psychologytoday.com/articles/200212/the-power-love [Accessed 23 March 2010].

McGrath, M. (200?) *Subliminal Messages And Advertising.* ArticleSnatch. Available at http://www.articlesnatch.com/Article/Subliminal-Messages-And-Advertising/377875 and http://www.personal-development.info/subliminals.html [Accessed 26 March 2010].

Merriam-Webster's Collegiate Dictionary (2003) II edition.

Nightingale, E. *In:* ThinkExist. Available at: http://thinkexist.com/quotation/whatever_we_plant_in_our_subconscious_mind_and/252405.html [Accessed 26 March 2010].

Norville, D. (2007) *Thank You Power. Making The Science of Gratitude Work for You.* Nashville, Tennesse, Thomas Nelson Inc.

Owens, T. M. (200?) Happiness Comes form Within. Available at: http://www.e-t-c.me.uk/pdf/Artricle%203%20-HAPPINESS%20-%20Personal%20Power.pdf [Accessed 26 March 2010].

Oxford American Dictionary (2003) United States, Oxford University Press.

Paddison, S. (ed) (1998) *Hidden Power of the Heart: Discovering an Unlimited Source of Intelligence.* HeartMath.

Paige, S. *In:* ThinkExist. Available at: http://thinkexist.com/quotation/work_like_you_don-t_need_the_money-love_like_you/219326.html [Accessed 23 March 2010].

Penczak, C. (2009) *The Inner Temple of Witchcraft.* Woodbury, Llewellyn Publications.

Physorg (2008) Study Shows Compassion Meditation Changes the Brain. Available at: http://www.physorg.com/news161355537.html [Accessed 20 March 2010].

Physorg (2009) Meditation Increases Brain Gray Matter. Available at: http://www.physorg.com/news161355537.html [Accessed 20 March 2010].

Plato. (2008, first published 1871) *Symposium.* Forgotten Books. Available at: http://books.google.com/books/p/pub-4297897631756504?id=MxxrJeniGDwC&printsec=frontcover&dq=symposium&ei=eBayS

8bfHY7uM_Hj4fwE&cd=1#v=onepage&q=&f=false [Accessed 30 March 2010].

Power, C. (2010) The Top 10 Relationship Myths of All Time. Available at: www.sydneycounsellor.com [Accessed 22 March 2010].

Pratakins, A. R.(1992). The cargo-cult science of subliminal persuasion. *Skeptical Inquirer*, 16, pp260-272.

Premji, F. (2009) 100 Benefits of Meditation. I Need Motivation. Available at: http://www.ineedmotivation.com/blog/2008/05/100-benefits-of-meditation/ [Accessed 20 March 2010].

Raikes, C. (2005) Love Yourself First – I'm Happy, You're Happy, We're All Happy! Available at: http://ezinearticles.com/?Love-Yourself-First—Im-Happy,-Youre-Happy,-Were-All-Happy!&id=61328 [Accessed 22 March 2010].

Religion 'linked to happy life' (2008) BBC News of 18 March. Available at: http://news.bbc.co.uk/2/hi/health/7302609.stm [Accessed 26 March 2010].

Rettig, J. (2008) Power of Gratitude. Law of Attraction Outlined. Available at: http://www.law-of-attraction-outlined.com/power-of-gratitude.html [Accessed 5 November 2009].

Rinpoche, S. (1994) *The Tibetan Book of Living and Dying.* HarperOne.

Robbins, T. *In:* ThinkExist. Available at: http://thinkexist.com/quotation/we_waste_time_looking_for_the_perfect_lover/225254.html [Accessed 30 March 2010].

Robinson, D. M. and Fluck, E. J. (ed) (1979) *A Study of the Greek Love-Names.* Arno Press.

Rumi, J. *In:* Ergin, N. O. and Johnson, W. (2006) *The Forbidden Rumi: The Suppressed Poems of Rumi on Love, Heresy, and Intoxication.* Rochester, Vermont, Inner Transitions.

Ryan, M. J. (1999) *Attitudes of Gratitude. How to Give and Receive Joy Every Day of Your Life.* Boston, Conari Press.

Safire, W. and Safir, L. (1989) *Words of Wisdom. More Good Advice.* New York, Simon&Schuster.

San Francisco Books (2010) Books of Love. Available at: http://www.sfheart.com/lovebooks.html [Accessed 22 March 2010].

Sasson, R. (200?) Happiness is Within Us. Available at: http://www.successconsciousness.com/index_00001f.htm [Accessed 26 March 2010].

Stinson, S. (2005) *The Angels Have a Message for You. It's Time to Love Yourself!* Oxford, Trafford Publishing.

Subliminal images impact on brain (2007) BBC News of 9th March. Available at: http://news.bbc.co.uk/2/hi/health/6427951.stm [Accessed 26 March 2010].

Talmadge, C. L. (2008) Love: The Ultimate Vibration. Available at: http://www.articlesbase.com/new-age-articles/love-the-ultimate-vibration-494436.html [Accessed 22 March 2010].

Tan, E. (2006) Seven States of Matter – Everything is Mind. Mind Reality. Available at: http://www.mindreality.com/seven-states-of-matter-everything-is-mind [Accessed 23 March 2010].

The Bible: The New King James Version of The Bible. (1982) Thomas Nelson.

The Dhammapada (1973). London, The Penguin Group.

The Sunan Method (2003) The Sunan Society. Available at: http://www.sunan.com/ [Accessed 22 March 2010].

ThinkExist (200?) Available at: http://thinkexist.com/quotation/laugh-as-much-as-you-breathe-and-love-as-long-as/354603.html [Accessed 23 March 2010].

Three Initiates. (2008, first published 1908) *The Kybalion, The Hermetic Philosophy*. Forgotten Books. Available at: http://books.google.com/books/p/pub-4297897631756504?id=8E_Nfq0_kIwC&printsec=frontcover&dq=kybalion&ei=I-GoS52WC5TaMZfNhdcM&cd=I#v=onepage&q=&f=false [Accessed 23 March 2010].

Trine, R. W. (2008, first published 1910) *In Tune with the Infinite: Fullness of Peace, Power and Plenty*. Forgotten Books. Available at: http://books.google.com/books/p/pub-4297897631756504?id=JkAQTdFcNPQC&printsec=frontcover&dq=In+Tune+with+the+Infinite&ei=a9SsS4CYOIWyNIvtzc8M&hl=it&cd=I#v=onepage&q=&f=false [Accessed 26 March 2010].

University of Michigan (200?) Subliminal. Available at: http://www.umich.edu/~onebook/pages/frames/usesSet.html [Accessed 26 March 2010].

Violet's View (2009) *Gratitude and Your Power to Create*. Hubpages. Available at: http://hubpages.com/hub/Gratitude-The-Secret-of-a-Successful-LIfe [Accessed 20 March 2010].

Wallace, B. A. (2007) *Contemplative Science*. New York, Columbia University Press.

Watkins, P.C. *et al* (2004) Counting your blessings: positive memories among grateful persons. *Current Psychology: Developmental, Learning, Personality, Social*.

Wattles, W. D. (2008) *The Science of Getting Rich*. Forgotten Books. Available at: http://books.google.com/books/p/pub-4297897631756504?id=z3VIX0GInakC&printsec=frontcover&dq=The+Science+of+Getting+Rich&ei=0I6mS5vmOoOGyASbqYi_CA&cd=I#v=onepage&q=&f=false [Accessed 21 March 2010].

Weber, T. (2010) Happiness revisited: Does money make us happy after all? BBC News of 28 Jan. Available at: http://news.bbc.co.uk/2/hi/business/8484368.stm [Accessed 26 March 2010].

Wikipedia (2010) All You Need is Love. Available at: http://en.wikipedia.org/wiki/All_You_Need_Is_Love [Accessed 30 March 2010].

Wikipedia (2010) FedEx. Available at: http://it.wikipedia.org/wiki/FedEx [Accessed 26 March 2010].

Wikipedia (2010) Gratitude. Available at: http://en.wikipedia.org/wiki/Gratitude [Accessed 20 March 2010].

Wikipedia (2010) Happiness. Available at: http://en.wikipedia.org/wiki/Happiness [Accessed 26 March 2010].

Wikipedia (2010) Halloween. Available at: http://en.wikipedia.org/wiki/Halloween [Accessed 20 March 2010].

Wikipedia (2010) Hermeticism. Available at: http://en.wikipedia.org/wiki/Hermeticism [Accessed 24 March 2010].

Wikipedia (2010) Instances of Subliminal Message. Available at: http://en.wikipedia.org/wiki/Instances_of_subliminal_message [Accessed 26 March 2010].

Wikipedia (2010) Love. Available at: http://en.wikipedia.org/wiki/Love [Accessed 22 March 2010].

Wikipedia (2010) Love is All Around. Available at: http://en.wikipedia.org/wiki/Love_Is_All_Around_(The_Troggs_song) [Accessed 30 March 2010].

Wikipedia (2010) Love Styles. Available at: http://en.wikipedia.org/wiki/Love_styles [Accessed 22 March 2010].

Wikipedia (2010) Marriage. Available at: http://en.wikipedia.org/wiki/Marriage [Accessed 22 March 2010].

Wikipedia (2010) Meditation. Available at: http://en.wikipedia.org/wiki/Meditation [Accessed 20 March 2010].

Wikipedia (2010) Narcissism. Available at: http://en.wikipedia.org/wiki/Narcissism [Accessed 22 March 2010].

Wikipedia (2010) Placebo. Available at: http://en.wikipedia.org/wiki/Placebo [Accessed 26 March 2010].

Wikipedia (2010) Que Linda Manito. Available at: http://en.wikipedia.org/wiki/Que_Linda_Manito [Accessed 22 March 2010].

Wikipedia (2010) Stalactite. Available at: http://en.wikipedia.org/wiki/Stalactite [Accessed 26 March 2010].

Wikipedia (2010) Subliminal Stimuli. Available at: http://en.wikipedia.org/wiki/Subliminal_stimuli [Accessed 26 March 2010].

Wikipedia (2010) Symposium Plato. Available at: http://en.wikipedia.org/wiki/Symposium_(Plato) [Accessed 22 March 2010].

Wikipedia (2010) The Exorcist. Available at: http://en.wikipedia.org/wiki/The_Exorcist_(film) [Accessed 26 March 2010].

Wikipedia (2010) Triangular Theory of Love. Available at: http://en.wikipedia.org/wiki/Triangular_theory_of_love [Accessed 23 March 2010].

Wikipedia (2010) Virgin Group. Available at: http://it.wikipedia.org/wiki/Virgin_Group [Accessed 26 March 2010].

Wilde, O. (1906) *An Ideal Husband*. Boston, John W. Luce & Company.

Zaher, M. and Ozwald, J. (200?) The Extraordinary Magic of Self Love. Available at: http://www.trans4mind.com/counterpoint/index-spiritual/ozwald2.shtml [Accessed 22 March 2010].

Endnotes

1   Quote by Buddha *In: The Dhammapada* (1973) London, The Penguin Group, p35.

2   Holmes, O. W. *In:* ThinkExist. Available at: http://thinkexist. com/quotation/man-s_mind-once_stretched_by_a_new_idea-never/8182.html [Accessed 30 March 2010].

3   Quote by Buddha *In:* King, J. D. (2009) *World Transformation: A Guide to Personal Growth and Consciousness.* AuthorHouse UK Ltd., p296.

4   Quote by Buddha *In: The Dhammapada* (1973) London, The Penguin Group, p35.

5   Conan Doyle, A. (2010) A Scandal in Bohemia. *In: The Adventures of Sherlock Holmes.* CreateSpace, p3.

6   Ibid.

7   De Angeles, L. (2008) *Witchcraft: Theory and Practice.* Woodbury, Llewellyn Publications, pp4-5.

8   Rinpoche, S. (1994) *The Tibetan Book of Living and Dying.* Harper-One, p56.

9   Aubrey, A. (2005) Science Explores Meditation's Effect on Brain. Available at: http://www.npr.org/templates/story/story. php?storyId=4770779 [Accessed 20 March 2010].

10 Barbor, C. (2001) The Science of Meditation. *Psychology Today.* Available at: http://www.psychologytoday.com/articles/200105/the-science-meditation [Accessed 20 March 2010].

11 Ibid.

12 Physorg (2009) Meditation Increases Brain Gray Matter. Available at: http://www.physorg.com/news161355537.html [Accessed 20 March 2010].

13 Barbor, C. (2001) The Science of Meditation. *Psychology Today.* Available at: http://www.psychologytoday.com/articles/200105/the-science-meditation [Accessed 20 March 2010].

14 Physorg (2008) Study Shows Compassion Meditation Changes the Brain. Available at: http://www.physorg.com/news161355537.html [Accessed 20 March 2010].

15 Hughes, D. (200?) Meditation and Spirituality: An interview with Deepak Chopra. Share Guide. Available at: http://www.shareguide. com/Chopra2.html [Accessed 20 March 2010].

16 EOC Institute (200?) Instant Deep Meditation. Available at: http:// www.eocinstitute.org/brainwave_synchronization_s/47.htm [Accessed 20 March 2010].

17 Premji, F. (2009) 100 Benefits of Meditation. I Need Motivation. Available at: http://www.ineedmotivation.com/blog/2008/05/100-benefits-of-meditation/ [Accessed 20 March 2010]. Used by permission of Frederic Premji.

18 Wikipedia (2010) Meditation. Available at: http://en.wikipedia.org/ wiki/Meditation [Accessed 20 March 2010].

19 Wallace, B. A. (2007) *Contemplative Science*. New York, Columbia University Press, p81.

20 Flood, G. D. (1996) *An Introduction to Hinduism*. New York, Cambridge University Press, pp94–95.

21 Buckland, R. (2002) *Buckland's Complete Book of Witchcraft* ©. 2143 Wooddale Drive, Woodbury, MN 55125-2989. Llewellyn Worldwide, Ltd., p111. All rights reserved, used by permission of and with the best wishes of the publisher.

22 Barbor, C. (2001) The Science of Meditation. *Psychology Today*. Available at: http://www.psychologytoday.com/articles/200105/the-science-meditation [Accessed 20 March 2010].

23 Wikipedia (2010) Meditation. Available at: http://en.wikipedia.org/ wiki/Meditation [Accessed 20 March 2010].

24 Ülsever, E. (2010) Meditation [Picture]

25 Buckland, R. (2002) *Buckland's Complete Book of Witchcraft* ©. 2143 Wooddale Drive, Woodbury, MN 55125-2989. Llewellyn Worldwide, Ltd., p111. All rights reserved, used by permission of and with the best wishes of the publisher.

26 Penczak, C. (2009) *The Inner Temple of Witchcraft*. Woodbury, Llewellyn Publications, pp96-97.

27 Buckland, R. (2002) *Buckland's Complete Book of Witchcraft* ©. 2143 Wooddale Drive, Woodbury, MN 55125-2989. Llewellyn Worldwide, Ltd., p111. All rights reserved, used by permission of and with the best wishes of the publisher.

28 Ibid.

29   Quote by Buddha *In: The Dhammapada* (1973). London, The Penguin Group, p35.

30   De Angeles, L. (2008) *Witchcraft: Theory and Practice.* Woodbury, Llewellyn Publications, p50.

31   Demarco, S. (2006) *Witch in the Bedroom.* Woodbury, Llewellyn Publications, p85.

32   Ryan, M. J. (1999) *Attitudes of Gratitude. How to Give and Receive Joy Every Day of Your Life.* Boston, Conari Press, p14.

33   Wikipedia (2010) Halloween. Available at: http://en.wikipedia.org/wiki/Halloween [Accessed 20 March 2010].

34   Emmons, R. A. and McCullough, M. E. (2004) *The Psychology of Gratitude.* New York, Oxford University Press, p3.

35   Ibid, p6.

36   Canfield, J. and Watkins, D. D. (2007) *Gratitude – A Daily Journal. Honor and Appreciate the Abundance in Your Life.* Florida, Health Communications, p3.

37   Wikipedia (2010) Gratitude. Available at: http://en.wikipedia.org/wiki/Gratitude [Accessed 20 March 2010].

38   Emmons, R. A. (2007) *Thanks! How the New Science of Gratitude Can Make You Happier.* New York, Houghton-Mifflin, p39.

39   Rettig, J. (2008) Power of Gratitude. Law of Attraction Outlined. Available at: http://www.law-of-attraction-outlined.com/power-of-gratitude.html [Accessed 5 November 2009].

40   Violet's View (2009) Gratitude and Your Power to Create. Hubpages. Available at: http://hubpages.com/hub/Gratitude-The-Secret-of-a-Successful-LIfe [Accessed 20 March 2010].

41   Ibid.

42   King, S. K. (2003) *The Little Pink Booklet of Aloha.* Hawaii, Aloha International. Used by permission of Serge Kahili King.

43   Ibid.

44   Violet's View (2009) Gratitude and Your Power to Create. Hubpages. Available at: http://hubpages.com/hub/Gratitude-The-Secret-of-a-Successful-LIfe [Accessed 20 March 2010].

45   Ibid.

46   Buddha. *In:* ThinkExist. Available at: http://thinkexist.com/quotation/let_us_rise_up_and_be_thankful-for_if_we_didn-t/199980.html [Accessed 30 March 2010].

47   Violet's View (2009) Gratitude and Your Power to Create. Hubpages. Available at: http://hubpages.com/hub/Gratitude-The-Secret-of-a-Successful-LIfe [Accessed 20 March 2010].

48   Lyubomirsky, S. (2007) *The How of Happiness. A New Approach to Getting the Life You Want.* United States, Penguin Books, pp92-95.

49   Fredrickson, B.L. *et al* (2003) What good are positive emotions in crises?: A prospective study of resilience and emotions following terrorist attacks on the United States in September II, 2001. *Journal of Personality and Social Psychology.*

50   Watkins, P.C. *et al* (2004) Counting your blessings: positive memories among grateful persons. *Current Psychology: Developmental, Learning, Personality, Social.*

51   Emmons, R. A. and McCullough M. E. (2003) Counting blessings versus burdens: An experimental investigation of gratitude and subjective well-being in daily life. *Journal of Personality and Social Psychology.*

52   Ryan, M. J. (1999) Attitudes of Gratitude. How to Give and Receive Joy Every Day of Your Life. Boston, Conari Press, p6.

53   Beattie, M. (2007) *Gratitude.* Minnesota, Hazelden Foundation.

54   Canfield, J. and Watkins, D. D. (2007) *Gratitude — A Daily Journal. Honor and Appreciate the Abundance in Your Life.* Florida, Health Communications, p3.

55   Norville, D. (2007) *Thank You Power. Making The Science of Gratitude Work for You.* Nashville, Tennesse, Thomas Nelson Inc., p21.

56   ACFNewSource (2006) Gratitude Theory. Available at: http://www.acfnewsource.org/religion/gratitude_theory.html [Accessed 20 March 2010].

57   Ibid.

58   Ibid.

59   Wattles, W. D. (2008) *The Science of Getting Rich.* Forgotten Books. Available at: http://books.google.com/books/p/pub-4297897631756504?id=z3VIX0GInakC&printsec=frontcover&dq=The+Science+of+Getting+Rich&ei=0I6mS5vmOoOGyASbqYi_CA&cd=I#v=onepage&q=&f=false [Accessed 2I March 2010], pp36-37.

60   Ibid.

61 Burke, C. (2006) The Inner-Power Emails. Life with Confidence. Available at: http://www.life-with-confidence.com/support-files/ inner_power_emails.pdf [Accessed 21 March 2010].

62 Manahan, R. (2007) The Power of the Written Word. Fortify Your Oasis. Available at: http://fortifyservices.blogspot.com/2007/06/ power-of-written-word.html [Accessed 21 March 2010].

63 Icke, D. (2005) *Infinite Love is The Only Truth, Everything Else is Illusion. Exposing the dreamworld we believe to be "real".* S.n.

64 Wikipedia (2010) Love is All Around. Available at: http://en.wikipedia. org/wiki/Love_Is_All_Around_(The_Troggs_song) [Accessed 30 March 2010].

65 Wikipedia (2010) All You Need is Love. Available at: http:// en.wikipedia.org/wiki/All_You_Need_Is_Love [Accessed 30 March 2010].

66 Oxford American Dictionary (2003) United States, Oxford University Press and Merriam-Webster's Collegiate Dictionary (2003) 11 edition.

67 Kristeller, P. O. (1980). *Renaissance Thought and the Arts: Collected Essays.* Princeton University Press, p53.

68 Mascaró, J. (2003). *The Bhagavad Gita.* New York, Penguin Classics, p181.

69 Wikipedia (2010) Love. Available at: http://en.wikipedia.org/wiki/ Love [Accessed 22 March 2010].

70 Ibid and Robinson, D. M. and Fluck, E. J. (ed) (1979) *A Study of the Greek Love-Names.* Arno Press.

71 San Francisco Books (2010) Books of Love. Available at: http://www.sfheart.com/lovebooks.html [Accessed 22 March 2010].

72 Gold, T. (2003) *What is Love?: A Simple Buddhist Guide to Romantic Happiness.* Singapore, Lionstead Press, p5.

73 Scripture taken from the New King James Version of The Bible. Copyright © 1982 by Thomas Nelson, Inc. Used by permission. All rights reserved.

74 Gray, P. et al (1993) What is Love? *Time Magazine,* 15 February. Available at: http://www.time.com/time/magazine/article/0,9171,977763,00. html [Accessed 22 March 2010].

75 Lee, J. (1973) *Colors of Love: An Exploration of the Ways of Loving.* New York, New Press. In: Wikipedia (2010) Love Styles. Available

at: http://en.wikipedia.org/wiki/Love_styles [Accessed 22 March 2010].

76   Hendrick, C. and Hendrick, S. (1986) A theory and method of love. *J of Personality and Social Psychology,* Vol50, February, pp392-402. *In:* Wikipedia (2010) Love Styles. Available at: http://en.wikipedia.org/wiki/Love_styles [Accessed 22 March 2010].

77   Wikipedia (2010) Unconditional Love. Available at: http://en.wikipedia.org/wiki/Unconditional_love [Accessed 22 March 2010].

78   Baer, G. (2009) What is Real Love? Real Love. Available at: http://www.reallove.com/about.asp [Accessed 22 March 2010] Used by permission of Greg Baer.

79   Ibid.

80   Loo, T. (2006) The Power of Giving Unconditional Love. EzineArticles. Available at: http://ezinearticles.com/?The-Power-of-Giving-Unconditional-Love&id=368427 [Accessed 22 March 2010] Used by permission of Tristan Loo.

81   Ibid.

82   Ibid.

83   Ibid.

84   Icke, D. (1996) *I am me, I am free: The Robot's Guide to Freedom.* Bridge of Love, p140.

85   Brother Veritus, The Art and Science of Unconditional Love. Unconditional Love. Available at: http://www.luisprada.com/Protected/Unconditional_Love.htm [Accessed 22 March 2010].

86   Baer, G. (2009) What is Real Love? Real Love. Available at: http://www.reallove.com/about.asp [Accessed 22 March 2010] Used by permission of Greg Baer.

87   Icke, D. (1996) *I am me, I am free: The Robot's Guide to Freedom.* Bridge of Love, p142.

88   Baer, G. (2009) What is Real Love? Real Love. Available at: http://www.reallove.com/about.asp [Accessed 22 March 2010] Used by permission of Greg Baer.

89   Ibid.

90   Paddison, S. (ed) (1998) *Hidden Power of the Heart: Discovering an Unlimited Source of Intelligence.* HeartMath.

91   Talmadge, C. L. (2008) Love: The Ultimate Vibration. Available at http://www.articlesbase.com/new-age-articles/love-the-ultimate-vibration-494436.html [Accessed 22 March 2010] Used by

permission of Candace Talmadge, author and energy healer, www.
sunan.com

92 Ibid.

93 Brother Veritus, *The Art and Science of Unconditional Love.*
Unconditional Love. Available at: http://www.luisprada.com/
Protected/Unconditional_Love.htm [Accessed 22 March 2010].

94 Keyes, K. (1993) *The Power of Unconditional Love: 21 Guidelines for*
Beginning, Improving and Changing your Most Meaningful Relationships.
Love Line Books.

95 Roberts, J. *In:* Guthrie, G. P. (2003) *1,600 Quotes & Pieces of Wisdom*
That Just Might Help You Out When You're Stuck in a Moment (and
can't get out of it!). Nebraska, iUniverse, p48.

96 Wikipedia (2010) Narcissism. Available at: http://en.wikipedia.org/
wiki/Narcissism [Accessed 22 March 2010].

97 Stinson, S. (2005) *The Angels Have a Message for You. It's Time to Love*
Yourself! Oxford, Trafford Publishing, p7.

98 Ibid.

99 Wilde, O. (1906) *An Ideal Husband.* Boston, John W. Luce &
Company, p76.

100 Isha. (2008) *Why Walk When You Can Fly? Soar Beyond Your Fears*
and Love Yourself and Others Unconditionally. California, New World
Library, pXIV.

101 Bourbeau, L. (2001) *Your Body's Telling You: Love Yourself! The most*
complete book on metaphysical causes of illnesses & diseases. Quebec,
Les Editions E.T.C. Inc, p20.

102 Ibid.

103 Carter-Scott, C. (1999) *If Love is a Game, These Are the Rules.* New
York, Random House, pp4-5.

104 Ibid.

105 Ibid.

106 Ibid.

107 Colby, A. (2007) Do You Love Yourself? Self Growth. Available at:
http://www.selfgrowth.com/articles/Do_You_Love_Yourself.html
[Accessed 22 March 2010] Used by permission of Annette Colby.

108 Raikes, C. (2005) Love Yourself First – I'm Happy, You're
Happy, We're All Happy! Available at: http://ezinearticles.
com/?Love-Yourself-First—Im-Happy,-Youre-Happy,-Were-All-

Happy!&id=61328 [Accessed 22 March 2010] Used by permission of Claire Raikes, Intuitive Soulpreneur, www.ClaireRaikes.com.

[109] Ibid.

[110] Ibid.

[111] Ibid.

[112] Carter-Scott, C. (1999) *If Love is a Game, These Are the Rules*. New York, Random House, p2.

[113] Ibid.

[114] Icke, D. (1996) *I am me, I am free: The Robot's Guide to Freedom*. Bridge of Love, p141.

[115] Ball, L. *In:* Safire, W. and Safir, L. (1989) *Words of Wisdom. More Good Advice*. New York, Simon&Schuster, p345.

[116] Bourbeau, L. (2001) *Your Body's Telling You: Love Yourself! The most complete book on metaphysical causes of illnesses & diseases*. Quebec, Les Editions E.T.C. Inc, p12.

[117] Ibid.

[118] Wikipedia (2010) Masaru Emoto. Available at: http://en.wikipedia.org/wiki/Masaru_Emoto [Accessed 22 March 2010].

[119] Emoto, M. (2003) *The True Power of Water. Healing And Discovering Ourselves*. New York, Atria Books, p6.

[120] Emoto, M. (200?)*The Message from Water. Children's Book*. Emoto Peace Project. Available at: http://emotoproject.org [Accessed 22 March 2010] p8.

[121] Emoto, M. (2005) *The Hidden Messages in Water*. New York, Atria Books, pXXIV.

[122] Ibid, pXXV.

[123] Emoto, M. Thank You [Photograph] Authorization number: Office Masaru Emoto 100220733.

[124] Emoto, M. You Make Me Sick [Photograph] Authorization number: Office Masaru Emoto 100220733.

[125] Ibid, pXXVI.

[126] Emoto, M. (2007) *The Miracle of Water*. New York, Atria Books, pIX.

[127] Emoto, M. (200?)*The Message from Water. Children's Book*. Emoto Peace Project. Available at: http://emotoproject.org [Accessed 22 March 2010] pp24-25.

[128] Emoto, M. (2003) *The True Power of Water. Healing And Discovering Ourselves*. New York, Atria Books, p15.

129 Zaher, M. and Ozwald, J. (200?) The Extraordinary Magic of Self Love. Available at: http://www.trans4mind.com/counterpoint/index-spiritual/ozwald2.shtml [Accessed 22 March 2010] Used by permission of Margot Zaher, www.supermanifestor.com

130 Shoffstall, V. A. In: Canfield, J. and Hansen, M. V. (1995) A 2nd Helping of Chicken Soup for the Soul: 101 More Stories to Open the Heart and Rekindle the Spirit. Florida, Health Communications, p282.

131 Wikipedia (2010) Que Linda Manito. Available at: http://en.wikipedia.org/wiki/Que_Linda_Manito [Accessed 22 March 2010].

132 Maine, M. (2005) 20 Ways to Love Your Body!! National Eating Disorders Association. Available at http://www.nationaleatingdisorders.org/nedaDir/files/documents/handouts/20WaysTo.pdf [Accessed 22 March 2010] Used by permission of NEDA.

133 Corbin, K. (2007) The Magic of Self-Love. EzineArticles. Available at: http://ezinearticles.com/?The-Magic-of-Self-Love&id=749500 [Accessed 22 March 2010] Used by permission of Kate Corbin.

134 Zaher, M. and Ozwald, J. (200?) The Extraordinary Magic of Self Love. Available at: http://www.trans4mind.com/counterpoint/index-spiritual/ozwald2.shtml [Accessed 22 March 2010] Used by permission of Margot Zaher, www.supermanifestor.com

135 Ibid.

136 Ibid.

137 Robbins, T. In: ThinkExist. Available at: http://thinkexist.com/quotation/we_waste_time_looking_for_the_perfect_lover/225254.html [Accessed 30 March 2010].

138 Mauchline, P. (200?) The Perfect Partner. Available at www.artofloving.com [Accessed 22 March 2010] Used by permission of Paul Mauchline.

139 Ibid.

140 Ibid.

141 Ibid.

142 Icke, D. (1996) I am me, I am free: The Robot's Guide to Freedom. Bridge of Love, pp180-181.

143 Ibid.

144 Wikipedia (2010) Symposium Plato. Available at: http://en.wikipedia.org/wiki/Symposium_(Plato) [Accessed 22 March 2010].

145 Plato. (2008, first published 1871) Symposium. Forgotten Books. Available at: http://books.google.com/books/p/pub-

4297897631756504?id=MxxrJeniGDwC&printsec=frontcover&dq=
symposium&ei=eBayS8bfHY7uM_Hj4fwE&cd=1#v=onepage&q=&
f=false [Accessed 30 March 2010], pp22-24.

[146] Demarco, S. (2006) *Witch in the Bedroom*. Woodbury, Llewellyn Publications, pp69-73.

[147] Ibid.

[148] Byron, B. G. and Marchand, L. A. (1975) *Wedlock's the devil: 1814-1815*. United States, s.n., p239.

[149] Wikipedia (2010) Marriage. Available at: http://en.wikipedia.org/wiki/Marriage [Accessed 22 March 2010].

[150] Buckland's Complete Book of Witchcraft © 2002 by Raymond Buckland. (Page 137) Llewellyn Worldwide, Ltd. 2143 Wooddale Drive, Woodbury, MN 55125-2989. All rights reserved, used by permission of and with the best wishes of the publisher.

[151] Power, C. (2010) The Top 10 Relationship Myths of All Time. Available at: www.sydneycounsellor.com [Accessed 22 March 2010] Used by permission of Clinton Power.

[152] Rumi, J. *In*: Ergin, N. O. and Johnson, W. (2006) *The Forbidden Rumi: The Suppressed Poems of Rumi on Love, Heresy, and Intoxication.* Rochester, Vermont, Inner Transitions.

[153] ThinkExist (200?) Available at: http://thinkexist.com/quotation/laugh-as-much-as-you-breathe-and-love-as-long-as/354603.html [Accessed 23 March 2010].

[154] Wikipedia (2010) Triangular Theory of Love. Available at: http://en.wikipedia.org/wiki/Triangular_theory_of_love [Accessed 23 March 2010]. Used by permission of Prof Sternberg.

[155] Ibid, image used by permission of Prof Sternberg.

[156] Lynch, C. and Daniels, V. (2000) Patterns of Relationships. Available at: http://www.sonoma.edu/users/d/daniels/lynch.html [Accessed 23 March 2010] Used by permission of Victor Daniels.

[157] Quote by Rutkowska, A.

[158] Dr Seuss (1959) *Happy Birthday to You!* Party Edition. New York, Random House.

[159] McGrath, E. (2002) The Power of Love. *Psychology Today*. Available at: http://www.psychologytoday.com/articles/200212/the-power-love [Accessed 23 March 2010].

[160] Icke, D. (1996) *I am me, I am free: The Robot's Guide to Freedom.* Bridge of Love p166.

161 Buckland's Complete Book of Witchcraft © 2002 by Raymond Buckland. (Page 237) Llewellyn Worldwide, Ltd. 2143 Wooddale Drive, Woodbury, MN 55125-2989. All rights reserved, used by permission of and with the best wishes of the publisher.

162 Paraphrased quote by Paige, S. *In:* ThinkExist. Available at: http://thinkexist.com/quotation/work_like_you_don-t_need_the_money-love_like_you/219326.html [Accessed 23 March 2010].

163 Einstein, A. *In:* ThinkExist. Available at: http://thinkexist.com/quotation/reality_is_merely_an_illusion-albeit_a_very/15556.html [Accessed 23 March 2010].

164 Wikipedia (2010) Hermeticism. Available at: http://en.wikipedia.org/wiki/Hermeticism [Accessed 24 March 2010].

165 Three Initiates. (2008, first published 1908) *The Kybalion, The Hermetic Philosophy*. Forgotten Books. Available at: http://books.google.com/books/p/pub-4297897631756504?id=8E_Nfq0_kIwC&printsec=frontcover&dq=kybalion&ei=I-GoS52WC5TaMZfNhdcM&cd=1#v=onepage&q=&f=false [Accessed 23 March 2010], p11.

166 Ibid, pp32-38.

167 Ibid, pp57-68.

168 Ibid, pp69-74.

169 Ibid, pp75-80.

170 Ibid, pp81-87.

171 Ibid, pp88-94.

172 Ibid, pp95-110.

173 Tan, E. (2006) Seven States of Matter – Everything is Mind. Mind Reality. Available at: http://www.mindreality.com/seven-states-of-matter-everything-is-mind [Accessed 23 March 2010] Used by permission of Enoch Tan.

174 Dr Quantum – Double Slit Experiment (2010). BBC5.TV. Available at: http://news.bbc5.tv/story/dr-quantum-double-slit-experiment [Accessed 23 March 2010].

175 Einstein, A. *In:* Caesar, V. and Caesar, C.A. (2006) *The High Achiever's Guide to Happiness*. California, Corwin Press, p105.

176 Larson, C. D. (2008, first published 1912) *Your Forces and How to Use Them*. Forgotten Books. Available at: http://books.google.com/books/p/pub-4297897631756504?id=Q6UgNYp1HigC&printsec=frontcover&dq=Your+Forces+and+How+to+Use+Them&ei=OO

aoS9SsGZWQMoCmycYM&hl=it&cd=1#v=onepage&q=&f=false [Accessed 23 March 2010], p56.

177 Ibid, p56.

178 Ibid, p57.

179 Ibid, p69.

180 Ibid, p71.

181 Hamblin, H. T. (2008, first published 1923) *Dynamic Thought: Harmony, Health, Success, Achievement*. Forgotten Books. Available at: http://books.google.com/books/p/pub-4297897631756504?id=w 5uXOSU2rMkC&printsec=frontcover&dq=Dynamic+Thought:+H armony,+Health,+Success,+Achievement&ei=BeeoS465F420MN3 eraYM&hl=it&cd=1#v=onepage&q=&f=false [Accessed 23 March 2010], p69.

182 Ibid, pp69-70.

183 Ibid, p70.

184 Ibid, p70.

185 Ibid, p70.

186 Ibid, p70.

187 Ibid, p71.

188 Ibid, pp71-72.

189 Ibid, p72.

190 Abraham-Hicks. (2005) Excerpted from the workshop in Washington, DC on Saturday, May 7th. *In:* Gaia Community. Available at: http://www.gaia.com/quotes/abraham_hicks [Accessed 24 March 2010].

191 Kirtikar, M. (2006) Energy and Vibration. Available at: http:// ezinearticles.com/?Energy-and-Vibration&id=356857 [Accessed 24 March 2010] Used by permission of Margo Kirtikar, www. margokirtikar.com, www.mindempowerment.net

192 Ibid.

193 Ibid.

194 Ibid.

195 Abraham-Hicks. (2002) Excerpted from the workshop in El Paso, TX on Thursday, March 28th. *In:* Gaia Community. Available at: http://www.gaia.com/quotes/abraham_hicks [Accessed 24 March 2010].

196 Abraham-Hicks. (1999) Excerpted from the workshop in Portland, OR on Sunday, July 11th. *In:* Personal Development Forum. Available

at: http://www.personaldevelopmentforum.com/abraham-hicks. html [Accessed 24 March 2010].

[197] Atkinson, W. W. (2008, first published 1918) *The Secret Doctrine of the Rosicrucians*. Forgotten Books. Available at: http://books. google.com/books/p/pub-4297897631756504?id=RlrhC_vEHXA C&printsec=frontcover&dq=The+Secret+Doctrine+of+the+Ro sicrucian&ei=fvSpS8bzJZ2uMov0tbYM&cd=1#v=onepage&q=T he%20Secret%20Doctrine%20of%20the%20Rosicrucian&f=false [Accessed 24 March 2010], p136.

[198] Ibid.

[199] Ibid, pp136-137.

[200] Ibid, p137.

[201] Ibid, p137.

[202] Ibid, p141.

[203] Ibid, pp141-142.

[204] Ibid, pp137-138.

[205] Ibid, p143.

[206] Wikipedia (2010) Chakra. Available at: http://en.wikipedia.org/wiki/ Chakra [Accessed 24 March 2010].

[207] Ibid.

[208] Ibid.

[209] Koyre, A. (2008, first published 1913) *Mahanirvana Tantra: Tantra of the Great Liberation*. Forgotten Books. Available at: http://books. google.com/books/p/pub-4297897631756504?id=FYaIQbFtPmYC &printsec=frontcover&dq=Mahanirvana+Tantra:+Tantra+of+the +Great+Liberation&ei=LPapS4y9O4ruNMeF4awM&hl=it&cd=1- #v=onepage&q=&f=false [Accessed 24 March 2010], pp29-34 and Wikipedia (2010) Chakra. Available at: http://en.wikipedia.org/wiki/ Chakra [Accessed 24 March 2010].

[210] Seven Chakras and spirituality symbols and men in lotus pose. [Image] BigStock. Available at: http://www.bigstockphoto.com/ image-3011050/stock-vector-chakras-symbols [Accessed 24 March 2010].

[211] Carberry, S. (2005) Chakra Balancing Visualization Exercise. The Body Mind and Soul. Available at: http://www.thebodymindandsoul. com/chakra-balancing-guided-meditation-exercise.htm [Accessed 24 March 2010] Used by permission of Sue Carberry.

212 Buddha. *In*: ThinkExist. Available at: http://thinkexist.com/quotation/every_human_being_is_the_author_of_his_own_health/200690.html [Accessed 26 March 2010].

213 Holmes, E. S. (2008, first published 1926) *The Science of Mind*. Forgotten Books. Available at: http://books.google.com/books/p/pub-4297897631756504?id=Y45W8kh25FMC&printsec=frontcover&dq=The+Science+of+Mind&ei=4rusS5XyGpSoNtTApboM&cd=1#v=onepage&q=&f=false [Accessed 26 March 2010], p103.

214 Ibid, p105.

215 Ibid, p122.

216 Ibid, p122.

217 Ibid, p122.

218 Ibid, p139.

219 Ibid, p117.

220 Ibid, p119.

221 Ibid, p123.

222 Ibid, p113.

223 Ibid, p124.

224 Ibid, p113.

225 Ibid, p116.

226 Ibid, p140.

227 Ibid, p12.

228 Ibid, p126.

229 Ibid, p128.

230 Ibid, p129.

231 Ibid, p129.

232 Ibid, p130.

233 Ibid, p132.

234 Ibid, p119.

235 Ibid, p124.

236 Atkinson, W. W. (2008, first published 1918) *The Secret Doctrine of the Rosicrucians*. Forgotten Books. Available at: http://books.google.com/books/p/pub-4297897631756504?id=RlrhC_vEHXAC&printsec=frontcover&dq=The+Secret+Doctrine+of+the+Rosicrucian&ei=fvSpS8bzJZ2uMov0tbYM&cd=1#v=onepage&q=The%20Secret%20Doctrine%20of%20the%20Rosicrucian&f=false [Accessed 24 March 2010], p144.

237 Ibid.

238 Wikipedia (2010) Placebo. Available at: http://en.wikipedia.org/wiki/Placebo [Accessed 26 March 2010].

239 Ibid.

240 Ibid.

241 Nightingale, E. *In:* ThinkExist. Available at: http://thinkexist.com/quotation/whatever_we_plant_in_our_subconscious_mind_and/252405.html [Accessed 26 March 2010].

242 Freud, S. *In:* QuotationsBook. Available at: http://quotationsbook.com/quote/26442/ [Accessed 26 March 2010].

243 Hill, N. (2008, first published 1938) *Think and Grow Rich.* Forgotten Books. Available at: http://books.google.com/books/p/pub-4297897631756504?id=c86H36mgiM4C&printsec=frontcover&dq=Think+and+Grow+Rich&ei=h76sS7a_L4TANpillcwM&hl=it&cd=1#v=onepage&q=&f=false [Accessed 26 March 2010], p204.

244 Ibid, p204.

245 Ibid, p204.

246 McGrath, M. (200?) *Subliminal Messages And Advertising.* ArticleSnatch. Available at http://www.articlesnatch.com/Article/Subliminal-Messages-And-Advertising/377875 and http://www.personal-development.info/subliminals.html [Accessed 26 March 2010]. Used by permission of ArticleSnatch Administrator.

247 Ülsever, E. (2010) Subliminal Messages [Picture].

248 Wikipedia (2010) Subliminal Stimuli. Available at: http://en.wikipedia.org/wiki/Subliminal_stimuli [Accessed 26 March 2010].

249 Pratakins, A. R.(1992). The cargo-cult science of subliminal persuasion. *Skeptical Inquirer,* 16, pp260-272.

250 Wikipedia (2010) Subliminal Stimuli. Available at: http://en.wikipedia.org/wiki/Subliminal_stimuli [Accessed 26 March 2010] and Karremans, J.C. *et al* (2006) Beyond Vicary's fantasies: The impact of subliminal priming and brand choice. *Journal of Experimental Social Psychology,* 42, pp792-798.

251 Bermeitinger, C. *et al* (2009) The hidden persuaders break into the tired brain. *Journal of Experimental Social Psychology,* 45, pp320-326.

252 Karremans, J.C. *et al* (2006) Beyond Vicary's fantasies: The impact of subliminal priming and brand choice. *Journal of Experimental Social Psychology,* 42, pp792-798.

253 Key, W. B. (1973) *Subliminal seduction: Ad media's manipulation of a not so innocent America.* Englewood Cliffs, NJ, Prentice-Hall.

254 Byrne, D. (1959). The effect of a subliminal food stimulus on verbal responses. *Journal of Applied Psychology, 43,* pp249–252.

255 Ibid.

256 Wikipedia (2010) Instances of Subliminal Message. Available at: http://en.wikipedia.org/wiki/Instances_of_subliminal_message [Accessed 26 March 2010].

257 Democrats smell campaign rat (2010) BBC News of 12th Sept. Available at: http://news.bbc.co.uk/2/hi/in_depth/americas/2000/us_elections/election_news/921830.stm [Accessed 26 March 2010].

258 Krosnick, J. A. *et al* (1992). Subliminal Conditioning of Attitudes. *Personality and Social Psychology Bulletin, 18: 152.*

259 Subliminal images impact on brain (2007) BBC News of 9th March. Available at: http://news.bbc.co.uk/2/hi/health/6427951.stm [Accessed 26 March 2010].

260 Ibid.

261 Ibid.

262 Ibid.

263 Wikipedia (2010) Subliminal Stimuli. Available at: http://en.wikipedia.org/wiki/Subliminal_stimuli [Accessed 26 March 2010].

264 Disney recalls video over 'nude image' (1999) BBC News of Jan 9th Available at: http://news.bbc.co.uk/2/hi/entertainment/251532.stm [Accessed 26 March 2010].

265 Ibid.

266 Ibid.

267 Wikipedia (2010) The Exorcist. Available at: http://en.wikipedia.org/wiki/The_Exorcist_(film) [Accessed 26 March 2010].

268 Wikipedia (2010) FedEx. Available at: http://it.wikipedia.org/wiki/FedEx [Accessed 26 March 2010].

269 DavidIcke Forum (2010) Available at: http://www.davidicke.com/forum/showthread.php?p=1058648861 [Accessed 26 March 2010].

270 Wikipedia (2010) Virgin Group. Available at: http://it.wikipedia.org/wiki/Virgin_Group [Accessed 26 March 2010].

271 Wikipedia (2010) Instances of Subliminal Message. Available at: http://en.wikipedia.org/wiki/Instances_of_subliminal_message [Accessed 26 March 2010].

272 Wikipedia (2010) Subliminal Stimuli. Available at: http://en.wikipedia.org/wiki/Subliminal_stimuli [Accessed 26 March 2010].

273 University of Michigan (200?) Subliminal. Available at: http://www. umich.edu/~onebook/pages/frames/usesSet.html [Accessed 26 March 2010].

274 Greenwald A. *et al* (1991). Double-Blind Test of Subliminal Self-Help Audtiotapes. *American Psychological Society, 2, no. 2.*

275 Icke, D. (2005) Infinite Love is The Only Truth, Everything Else is Illusion. Exposing the dreamworld we believe to be "real". S.n., p192.

276 Ibid, p192.

277 Holmes, E. S. (2008, first published 1926) *The Science of Mind.* Forgotten Books. Available at: http://books.google.com/books/p/ pub-4297897631756504?id=Y45W8kh25FMC&printsec=frontcove r&dq=The+Science+of+Mind&ei=4rusS5XyGpSoNtTApboM&cd=1 #v=onepage&q=&f=false [Accessed 26 March 2010], p14.

278 Ibid, p14.

279 Ibid, p15.

280 Ibid, p65.

281 Ibid, p66.

282 Ibid, p67.

283 Ibid, p68.

284 Ibid, p68.

285 Ibid, p94.

286 Ibid, p99.

287 Ibid, p125 and Wikipedia (2010) Stalactite. Available at: http:// en.wikipedia.org/wiki/Stalactite [Accessed 26 March 2010].

288 Ibid, p125.

289 Ibid, p166.

290 Ibid, p170.

291 Ibid, p205.

292 Ibid, p205.

293 Ibid, p205.

294 Ibid, p206.

295 Ibid, p206.

296 Ibid, p207.

297 Trine, R. W. (2008, first published 1910) *In Tune with the Infinite: Fullness of Peace, Power and Plenty.* Forgotten Books. Available at: http://books.google.com/books/p/pub-4297897631756504?id=JkA QTdFcNPQC&printsec=frontcover&dq=In+Tune+with+the+Infinit

e&ei=a9SsS4CYOIWyNIvtzc8M&hl=it&cd=1#v=onepage&q=&f=fa lse [Accessed 26 March 2010], p119.

298 Ibid, p119.

299 Ibid, p119.

300 Ibid, pp120-121.

301 Ibid, p121.

302 Ibid, pp121-122.

303 Ibid, p122.

304 Ibid, pp122-123.

305 Ibid, p123.

306 Ibid, p123.

307 Ibid, p124.

308 Ibid, pp124-125.

309 Holmes, E. S. (2008, first published 1926) *The Science of Mind*. Forgotten Books. Available at: http://books.google.com/books/p/ pub-4297897631756504?id=Y45W8kh25FMC&printsec=frontcove r&dq=The+Science+of+Mind&ei=4rusS5XyGpSoNtTApboM&cd=1 #v=onepage&q=&f=false [Accessed 26 March 2010], p22.

310 Ibid, p22.

311 Ibid, p22.

312 Ibid, pp24-25.

313 Ibid, pp25-26.

314 Ibid, p26.

315 Ibid, p26.

316 Ibid, p27.

317 Ibid, p36.

318 Ibid, p36.

319 Ibid, p36.

320 Ibid, p45.

321 Ibid, p46.

322 Ibid, p46.

323 Ibid, pp49-50.

324 Ibid, p54.

325 Ibid, p54.

326 Aristotle. *In:* ThinkExist. Available at: http://thinkexist.com/ quotation/happiness_is_the_meaning_and_the_purpose_of_ life/171697.html [Accessed 26 March 2010].

327   Cambridge Advanced Learner's Dictionary (2010) Happy. Available at: http://dictionary.cambridge.org/define.asp?key=35689&dict=CALD [Accessed 26 March 2010].

328   http://en.wikipedia.org/wiki/Happiness

329   Flora, C. (2009) The Pursuit of Happiness. *Psychology Today, Feb,* pp70-71.

330   Weber, T. (2010) Happiness revisited: Does money make us happy after all? BBC News of 28 Jan. Available at: http://news.bbc.co.uk/2/hi/business/8484368.stm [Accessed 26 March 2010].

331   Frey, B. S. and Stutzer, A. (Dec 2001). *Happiness and Economics.* Princeton University Press.

332   Ibid.

333   Easton, M. (2009) Map of The Week: Why Costa Rica is the happiest place. BBC of 4 July. Available at: http://www.bbc.co.uk/blogs/thereporters/markeaston/2009/07/map_of_the_week_why_costa_rica.html [Accessed 26 March 2010].

334   Ibid.

335   Ibid.

336   Ibid.

337   Ibid.

338   Ibid.

339   Ibid.

340   Ibid.

341   Ibid.

342   Wikipedia (2010) Happiness. Available at: http://en.wikipedia.org/wiki/Happiness [Accessed 26 March 2010].

343   Ibid.

344   Religion 'linked to happy life' (2008) BBC News of 18 March. Available at: http://news.bbc.co.uk/2/hi/health/7302609.stm [Accessed 26 March 2010].

345   Ibid.

346   Ibid.

347   Ibid.

348   Wikipedia (2010) Happiness. Available at: http://en.wikipedia.org/wiki/Happiness [Accessed 26 March 2010].

349   Loo, T. (2006) The Power of Unconditional Love. Available at: http://www.selfgrowth.com/articles/TristanLoo7.html [Accessed 26 March 2010].

350 Owens, T. M. (200?) Happiness Comes form Within. Available at: http://www.e-t-c.me.uk/pdf/Artricle%203%20-HAPPINESS%20-%20Personal%20Power.pdf [Accessed 26 March 2010]. Used by permission of Theresa M Owens.

351 Ibid.

352 Ibid.

353 Ibid.

354 Ibid.

355 Ibid.

356 Ibid.

357 Ibid.

358 Sasson, R. (200?) Happiness is Within Us. Available at: http://www.successconsciousness.com/index_00001f.htm [Accessed 26 March 2010]. Used by permission of Remez Sasson, http://www.successconsciousness.com

359 Ibid.

360 Ibid.

361 Ibid.

362 Ibid.

363 Ibid.

364 Edberg, H. (2007) How to Find Happiness: 7 Timeless Tips from the last 2500 Years. Available at: http://www.positivityblog.com/index.php/2007/09/26/how-to-find-happiness/ [Accessed 26 March 2010]; Sasson, R. (200?) Happiness is Within Us. Available at: http://www.successconsciousness.com/index_00001f.htm [Accessed 26 March 2010]. Used by permission of Remez Sasson, http://www.successconsciousness.com

365 Abraham-Hicks. (2004) Excerpted from the workshop in Washington, DC on Saturday, May 1st.

366 Maharishi Sadashiva Isham. *In:* Find-happiness. Available at: http://www.find-happiness.com/benefits-of-meditation.html [Accessed 11 April 2010].

Made in the USA
Lexington, KY
16 November 2010